staying POWER

Age-Proof Your Home for Comfort, Safety and Style

Rachel Adelson, M.A.

Sage Tree Publishing
Thornhill, Ontario
www.sagetreepublishing.com

Published by:

Sage Tree Publishing
66 Pantano Dr., Thornhill, Ontario L4J 0B2 Canada
www.sagetreepublishing.com

To order this book, please visit our website.

Managing Editor: Marla Markman

Cover design © 2012, www.leftrightcollaborative.com

Design: Jennifer Rogers Tyson

Interior design: 1106 Design, www.1106design.com

Library and Archives Canada Cataloguing in Publication
Adelson, Rachel
    Staying power : age-proof your home for comfort, safety and style / Rachel Adelson.
Includes index.
Issued also in electronic format.
ISBN 978-0-9878136-0-2

    1. Older people--Dwellings. 2. Dwellings--Remodeling. I. Title.
NA7195.A4A34 2012   728.0846   C2012-904481-4

Table of Contents

Disclaimer

This book is designed to provide information about the subject matter covered. It is sold with the understanding that the author and publisher are not engaged in rendering professional home contracting or health-care services.

Aging at home can be a complicated, unpredictable and lengthy transition that may require services and expertise outside the scope of this book. If such expert assistance is required, the services of a competent professional should be sought.

It is not the purpose of this handbook to supply all the information that is available to people aging at home or for those helping people age at home, but to complement, amplify and supplement other texts. For more information, see the Appendix.

Every effort has been made to make this book as complete and as accurate as possible. However, there may be mistakes, both typographical and in content. Therefore, this text should be used only as a general source of information on home modifications for older adults. Furthermore, this handbook contains information on aging at home only up to the printing date.

The purpose of this handbook is to educate. The author and publisher shall have neither liability nor responsibility to any person or entity with respect to any loss or damage caused or alleged to be caused directly or indirectly by the information contained in this book.

This book is dedicated to Alan and Pamela,
for helping me open new doors and believing
in the value of this book.

"Nothing in life is to be feared. It is only to be understood."

—Marie Curie

Introduction

Aging: A New Look at an Old Story

For less than the cost of a jar of wrinkle cream, you can get this book and actually *do* something proven to fight aging.

This handbook on healthy, productive aging at home is for you if, like me, you are a baby boomer or someone in the "sandwich generation" who wants to help your parents or other older relatives, friends or neighbors live independently with dignity in their own house or apartment.

It's also for you if you contemplate having, or already have, older relatives living with you or you live with them. Whether you worry about falls and fires, or simply want to make it easier for your loved ones to carry out their normal daily activities, you've come to the right place.

This book is for you, too, if you are noticing that life at home isn't as easy as it used to be, and you want to make it work again. Or you are planning ahead, hoping to prevent the injuries and discomfort you've seen other people suffer.

Whether you want to make changes for your own sake or for those you care about, more power to you for facing the need for change forthrightly.

Finally, this book is for the decorators and interior designers, handymen and contractors who work with older people and are in perhaps the best position to help them be safer and more comfortable. Many of you, I've found, take an active interest in this subject—whether it's because you're getting older, you also have parents aging at home, you know it's a growth market or you just plain care about your clients.

Real-estate professionals will find this book useful to help people decide whether to update or sell their homes, and to find new homes that better suit their needs. Geriatric care managers and social workers, home-health aides, occupational and physical therapists, and agencies that specialize in seniors will also find this material of interest.

Staying Power is a response to dramatic growth in the older population. As a society, we are just beginning to experience what it means to have and to house so many old, even very old, people—and we and they are not all going into assisted living, senior housing, retirement communities or nursing homes.

Most people live in their own homes by definition, whether it's the house in which they raised their kids or a post-downsizing house, townhouse, condo or apartment, owned or rented, developed for and marketed to older people or not. Anywhere you hang your hat is home.

Still, as the generation that once baby-proofed its homes prepares to age-proof the same, it needs to know how to respond to an older person's changing needs for comfort and safety, no matter what type of home. And as so many more of us transition into years, even decades, of potentially significant physical, sensory and cognitive change, we need to know how to help ourselves.

Aging: Consider the Alternative

Self-help starts with self-knowledge, and here, we're in luck. Gerontologists—people who study aging—have given us a great deal of information about the aging process.

To begin with, we know that people age in unique ways, influenced by some combination of genes, environment, and personal and social history. Given identical genes, for example, an 85-year-old woman who was a hungry migrant child in labor camps and didn't go past Grade 3 during the Great Depression may age differently than an 85-year-old woman who was well fed and well educated in a stable suburban home during the post-World War expansion.

The aging process varies in other ways, too. We all know people who were "born old" and those who stay perpetually youthful. Even within a single person, biological age might be lesser or greater than chronological age.

Despite all this variation, the tapestry of human aging has some common threads. For example, many of us get arthritis. We don't all get it, or get it at the same time or in the same joints, but many of us get it nonetheless because we all have joints and they show wear and tear. Similarly, many of us lose some ability to see, but the cause may vary from cataracts to macular degeneration.

No matter where, when or how we lived our younger days, there are some universals. To some degree, our senses dull; to some degree, we just slow down. On the plus side, we ride life's emotional roller coaster better than young people, have experience to burn and sometimes earn that age-old reputation for wisdom.

What else do we know about aging?

We know that some barriers to productive aging are on the outside. These are the practical and physical barriers that older people confront every day. You may already have noticed some of them: the crossing lights that change too fast, the tiny type on the medicine bottle, those sadistically high steps to climb onto the bus.

With external challenges to a secure and dignified old age growing more obvious, society is finally starting to crank itself up to address them. Yet change on the scale that is needed is likely to be slow. When it comes to public policy, helping the vulnerable tends to be low on the priority list. Meanwhile, we're all getting older. Who can wait?

In addition to external barriers to aging well, there is also an internal barrier—the sense that aging is *yucky* (in fancier terms, somehow repulsive).

The ugly truth is that society has tended to hide or mock old age, ignoring the growing number of people who are active, vital contributors to society well into their later years. Only recently, thanks to ads for prescription drugs, supplements and retirement funds, are we starting to see more positive images of people with gray hair and wrinkles.

Look, an achy knee is no fun, nor is trying to hear your dinner partner's conversation in today's noisy restaurants. Worse, though, is how those predicaments make us feel about aging. And that creates a double-whammy: Feeling bad *about* aging, on top of feeling bad *because* of aging. And that can send anyone into denial.

Yet denying the changes that come with age can actually make it harder to age well. It's like covering mirrors to get rid of wrinkles. Does. Not. Work. Negative attitudes about aging have even been linked to shorter life spans. In terms of the subject of this book—aging at home—those of us who acknowledge where we are at can more easily stay there in style.

So, make it your personal challenge to overcome the "ick" factor and do something proactive about aging. Knowledge is power. Start by reading this book and making a few simple adjustments around the house, updating it over time.

Graceful or even grateful acceptance of aging can actually help people retain more of the energy and capacity of youth. It turns out that aging well, like so many things, starts in the head.

A Word About "Aging"

Aging is a hot topic—and opinions on what to call it even hotter. Some people prefer the word "seniors" while others find it condescending. Some view "elderly" as a term of respect. Yet others think it connotes frailty and decay. Even the term "old" is open for debate, now that we must by necessity subdivide that age bracket, itself fairly arbitrary, into smaller and equally fairly arbitrary brackets such as the young-old, the oldest-old and the just plain old.

"Age" is a social construct; so is language. That said, to write this book, I had to use some kind of wording to describe the process of getting older in the way most of us think. I had to talk about old people, presenting "oldness" as a fact and not an insult.

Thus, the terms "older person" for individuals and "older people" for a population will be used, as well as "older adult" for variety and to remind us that older people are adults first, old second. These terms, along with the phrases "aging at home" and "aging in place," are currently used by respected academic, health and government institutions concerned with the subject of aging.

How to Use This Book

The easy-to-follow advice in *Staying Power* won't, in most cases, require you to hire a contractor (especially if you are one!), do major remodeling or get a permit, though it will raise those options and refer you to reliable resources.

The focus is on things you can do relatively quickly, without superior strength or elaborate tools. The process won't cost a million bucks or make your home look like a rehab ward.

Most important, this book will help you figure out how to respond to person-specific, situation-specific needs. To help you personalize your approach, *Staying Power* is organized by need and not by room, with two important exceptions for high-risk problems. Chapter 2, "The Stable Home: Preventing Falls," will help you prevent the No. 1 cause of accidental injury in older people. Chapter 3, "The Smoke-Free Home: Preventing Fires," puts the heat on the threat of home fires, an underestimated issue for the elderly.

Begin the journey to aging in place with Chapter 1, "The Thoughtful Home: Design for Living." Before you run out to the store or so much as change a single light bulb, learn common-sense principles of home safety and function as they apply to getting older. First do your "homework" so you can more wisely, systematically and economically improve any living space.

The rest of this book is dedicated to the nuts and bolts of making an older person's home a more pleasant, supportive and enriching place, addressing the most typical changes of normal, healthy aging.

Chapter 4, "The Easy Home: Function and Mobility," explains how to make everyday tasks, such as cooking and washing, easier and less energy-intensive by updating interiors and obtaining the right equipment for ease of use and movement.

Chapter 5, "The Sensitive Home: Eyes, Ears and More," offers simple, effective ways to compensate for sensory changes, including the less-often-discussed senses of touch, taste and smell.

Chapter 6, "The Holistic Home: Mind and Body," tells how to use the home environment to minimize the humbling impact of normal aging on the mind and maximize physical activity to boost cognitive abilities along with circulation, strength, flexibility and balance.

Chapter 7, "The Useful Home: Supportive Surroundings," reviews ways to quickly improve the safety of a home's outdoor and utility areas and presents a snapshot of emerging domestic technologies.

Chapter 8, "The Possible Home: Getting the Job Done," details, well, how to get the job of home modifications done and done right.

The Appendix includes a valuable, lengthy and comprehensive list of resources (in both the United States and Canada) and recommended reading, with more in-depth information for consumers and professionals alike. Because aging at home is not the best solution for every older person, some of these resources will help you uncover more suitable alternatives and make sound decisions.

Chapters 2 through 7 include "Let's Get Started" checklists with top tips for each major area of concern and "Let's Go Shopping" lists with do-it-yourself age-proofing tools you can find at housewares, hardware and home-health stores.

To keep the book price down, I've stuck mostly to text. If you'd like to see any item mentioned, from lever handle to roll-in shower or pocket door, do a quick image search on the Internet or visit a store or supplier (bricks and mortar, or online).

I hope you find this book helpful. My goal is to help you to see aging at home as a creative challenge, a chance to be caring and inventive, and above all an enjoyable way to make your home, or any home, a continued source of independence, vitality and joy.

Rachel Adelson
Thornhill, Ontario

Chapter 1

The Thoughtful Home: Design for Living

In their early 70s, John and Patricia pulled up stakes in the Midwest to be near their children and grandchildren in the Sunbelt. It was hard to find a house that wasn't too big to handle but still big enough for company, and they made compromises they weren't totally happy about. Still, they didn't see themselves in a retirement community.

Now Patricia's back bothers her, her knee kicks up when she tries to garden, and she'd rather make new friends than fix up the house. John's had cataract surgery, and once or twice he's slipped coming down the stairs. They had hoped to stay in their home until they were about 80, but they are starting to feel their staying power slipping away.

— ◆ —

Sound like anyone you know? The scenario above may describe your parents, your aunts and uncles or your friends' parents if you were born during the baby boom (1946 to 1964 in the United States or 1965 in Canada). In 2009, about 1 in every 8 Americans was 65 or older, according to the U.S. Administration on Aging.

With about 10,000 Americans turning 65 every day, the number of people 65 and older is projected to climb to more than 72 million people by the year 2030. Already, the "oldest-old" people—those 85 years and older—are the fastest-growing segment of the older population.

Older adults currently have the highest home-ownership rate of any age group. They usually live in the suburbs, especially the older suburbs that ring big cities. They fear the loss of independence, they want to stay home, and they are doing so—either in the place where they lived in their middle years, in the home they bought for retirement or with other family members (multigenerational housing is on the rise).

As recently as 2005, more than two-thirds of American households headed by older adults lived in ordinary, mixed-age communities, according to the National Association of Home Builders (NAHB). And throughout the United States and Canada, that situation is not going to change. For example, three-quarters of Canadians surveyed between the ages of 43 and 62 said they plan to stay home and just remodel, according to the Royal Bank of Canada.

Considering that people in their 40s and 50s are just starting to experience the physical realities of aging, the Canadians asked are merely being pragmatic. Change can start pretty young: Already, more than one-third of American households with people ages 55 to 64, and nearly half of households with people ages 65 to 74, report difficulty with at least one physical activity, such as dressing, walking, climbing the stairs, seeing or hearing, according to the NAHB.

Clearly, it's not just very old, very frail people who need help. But needing a little help with the stairs is vastly different from needing nursing care around the clock.

"It is a mistake to equate age and disability," writes gerontologist Michael Friedman of Columbia University. "The vast majority of people 65 and older are under 80, in decent health and mostly independent. Even at age 85, fewer than 50 percent of people are disabled and in need of help for basic functions," he adds, though they face steadily increasing odds of needing help.

Thus, the shifting landscape of aging has many of today's middle-aged people developing nontraditional "third acts" in life.

Many plan to work to some degree and stay active with their families and communities. They're beginning to reject the retirement model of wall-to-wall recreation— and, most important, they want to stay put.

The benefits of aging at home are obvious: greater independence, potentially lower cost, familiar and comfortable surroundings. Aging at home, also called aging in place, allows older people to remain in the communities they know, surrounded by people of all ages. Larger homes even allow for a family member or paid caregiver to provide live-in care.

(By the way, a sizable minority of older adults will have spent some time caring for grandchildren. Multigenerational living never really left us.)

Successful aging at home reduces the burden on hospitals and nursing or long-term care homes, freeing up resources for only the most seriously dependent and sick. The general reduction in health-care costs can be put to good use elsewhere, such as shifting funds to support home care, prevention and infrastructure.

Still, aging at home has its challenges. First, existing housing might not be suitable, with all those pesky stairs and such. Housing in general is built for the average, not the actual, family.

"Even though 9 out of 10 seniors 70 and over live in conventional housing, [it's] not designed to meet their changing needs, tastes and preferences," Harvard University's Joint Center for Housing Studies has reported.

Someone's specific needs may, whether slowly or suddenly, become poorly matched with a particular home. People often spend years modifying their homes to make them a custom fit.

As they age, people also become less able to meet the demands of living at home, including day-to-day maintenance and essential updates. It gets harder to change light bulbs and filters, get to the hardware store, and undertake or even supervise renovations.

Neglected maintenance of a longtime home can itself result in hazards. And often, its occupants are unable to call for help when they need it, whether "help" means a plumber or a paramedic.

There are other issues. When people remain in their homes, especially in suburban or rural single-family dwellings, their activity level may drop due to lack of transportation or nearby facilities. They may become isolated. There are gaps in supervision. On the other hand, when someone else has to check in often or live in to provide care, there's stress and perhaps an added cost.

Even with all this, people underestimate the odds of future illness or disability. Because we belong to an optimistic species, we have to force ourselves to push the pessimism button just a bit. We have to play "what if?" We need to develop alternatives (at least in theory) and to talk about the kinds of triggering events that might set a change in motion.

It helps to see things developmentally. After all, people don't suddenly turn "old," just the way kids don't suddenly become grown-ups, at least not in the legal sense. (Do you remember thinking about this? I do.) For most of us, gray hair comes in or falls out a bit at a time, maybe to keep us from going into shock.

So, whether you're a person "of a certain age," or you're among the oxymoronically named young-old (65 to 74), old (74 to 84), or the oldest-old (85+), life continues, as it did before, to be a series of overlapping changes, with older people tending to experience both gradual and sudden shifts in capability.

When it comes to housing, an informed understanding of aging allows people to be *more*, not *less*, in control of how and where they live.

"Successful aging in place demands that one's home and household products not only provide continued enjoyment and stimulation, [but] also support one's declining functional [abilities] and enhance one's quality of life," according to Transgenerational Design Matters, an education, research and advocacy group. That sums it up rather nicely.

A thoughtful review of the pluses and minuses of aging at home may help your parents, other loved ones or you (when the time comes) decide whether to stay home or move, be it to a smaller home or apartment, to retirement or senior housing, in with relatives, or to some other more suitable environment.

As part of this review, educate yourself about community services for aging in place. The relative availability of services might help swing the decision one way or another. Look, as well, to see if the grassroots "village" movement has made it to your area. These neighborhood-based groups, using a combination of volunteer and fee-based services, are springing up everywhere to help people age at home, supported by an umbrella Village to Village Network (see Appendix).

Emerging Alternatives

Innovative new housing types go beyond traditional retirement communities. It may take a little effort to seek them out, but the results could be rewarding.

For example, some older people are developing cohousing, which provides a balance between independence and community. Using existing housing or new construction, cohousing allows people to enjoy both privacy and regular companionship. Using a cooperative approach, residents can barter and share their expertise, such as trading painting for bookkeeping or sewing for specialty baking. They can also pool their resources to bring in outside help. This mutual-aid arrangement is a practical way to balance autonomy with the need for assistance and is, for many, preferable to living in an institution.

Cohousing can be developed by a group of compatible, like-minded friends or by people belonging to a social, faith or fraternal organization. It can also be sponsored by an outside group, such as a social service agency.

Meanwhile, leading builders have begun to forsake the bloated McMansions of boom times for the more compact, efficient houses (such as ranch styles, cottages and bungalows) sought by aging boomers and their achy knees. Smaller lot sizes and floor plans, the elimination of formal dining and living rooms in favor of big eat-in kitchens and roll-in showers instead of bathtubs sound appealing, especially for people headed to the kinds of popular retirement areas that will offer this type of new construction.

Indeed, the bigger challenge remains: to retrofit existing construction, update older homes, and turn suburban McMansions into group housing that accommodates the micro-communities for which, apparently, they were built. In addition, as multigenerational living becomes the norm, look for updated versions of the traditional "mother-in-law suite," "granny flat," or adjacent/joined elder cottage.

The recent economic downturn has accelerated a long-term shift back to traditional multigenerational housing, driven by the return of young adults to the family home but augmented significantly by the needs of elderly parents. Should a parent move in with you or vice versa, the advice in this book may help you all adapt the home in ways that suit both collective and individual needs, or at least hold informed negotiations.

In Good Company: Caregiver Concerns

A few years back, I conducted a pilot survey of people in their 40s and 50s to pinpoint some of the problems involved in caring for older people. It's impossible to generalize to the larger population what this 10-person (seven women, three men) sample of convenience reported, but some interesting issues arose.

These middle-aged professionals reported that they spent up to 10 hours a week helping to care for an older person(s), nearly all in their 80s, most living independently. As informal caregivers, these people relied on their powers of observation and complaints/requests by the people for whom they were making the home modifications, usually by themselves with varying degrees of uncertainty about whether they were doing it right.

Falls were ranked as the top home-safety issue, followed by stair and bathroom use. This reflected their personal experience, as more than half had dealt with falls in the previous year. It also reflects the general-population experience. According to the U.S. Centers for Disease Control and Prevention, 1 out of 3 adults age 65 and older falls each year. Among those people age 65 and older, falls are the leading cause of injury-related deaths as well as the most common cause of nonfatal injuries and hospital admissions for trauma (see Chapter 2 for tips on fall prevention).

Interestingly, everybody who knew about incidents of falling blamed behavior (either behavior alone, or behavior related to physical features of the home such as stairs). Nobody blamed home features alone for falls. Thus, a change in behavior was perceived by adult helpers as essential to preventing falls.

Fires were ranked low as a safety issue, contrary to the findings of safety professionals, some of whom say fires are the second most common home hazard for older people. Without studying a larger sample, it's impossible to speculate about the underestimation of fire hazards. In any case, kitchen and electrical fires occur with greater frequency than may be realized. To minimize that risk, steps should be taken both in the home and in behavior (see Chapter 3 for more on fire prevention).

Of home modifications made, grab bars and stair rails were most frequently mentioned. People who hired third parties to make changes felt they were trained to do the work correctly; however, they were less certain about the contractors' understanding of age-related safety needs (Chapters 2 and 4 may help).

At least half of the respondents said they would or might need further information in the future. To make more changes, most respondents said they would watch for signs of functional decline and attend to complaints from their loved ones (declining vision was often mentioned). Other cues to intervene included falls and accidents, failing memory, and a desire to stay home that could be fulfilled only if changes were made.

More than half of the respondents said the older person(s) resisted home modifications. The dominant reason was a belief that modifications diminish independence and autonomy, followed by residents not thinking they were needed, or saying the changes made them "feel old." A few older individuals thought modifications would be too expensive.

If concerns about independence and negative beliefs about aging block acceptance of modifications, then interventions could take those attitudes into account. Incorporating safety features into housing earlier in the life cycle, as well as in new construction, would make them less obviously tied to old age.

Finally, most people hadn't heard of any local "senior proofing" services. Most cited a lack of skill and time, plus distance, as reasons to hire someone else to modify a home. Many also saw value in using a "pro" or outside authority to get things done properly, avoid the expense of rework, and gain the trust of or convince the resident of the need for change (see Chapter 8 on how to get the job done).

In summary, the people surveyed were spending the equivalent of half to a whole workday every week helping people in their 80s to live independently. At least half made basic home-safety modifications, such as installing stair rails and grab bars, especially in the bathroom. Most of them correctly cited falls as the major safety problem for seniors, in part based on their experience. Most of them underestimated the risk of fire.

Older people were found to view home modifications as visible signs of decreased autonomy and independence, of an unseemly "old age." Some thought they weren't necessary. In other words, a reluctance or resistance to change was an overriding issue.

Does any of this sound familiar? Discussion of aging parents is increasingly dominating social discourse and causing chronic stress for caregivers, sometimes for decades. Although no one can fully appreciate your unique experience of helping relatives and friends in their latter-life journey, there are common themes. Knowledge is power. If you're reading this book, pat yourself on the back for giving yourself a road map for the journey ahead.

Planning for Change: Good Communication

You may be thinking about your own needs for that journey, or you may already be a caregiver or expecting to move into that role. You probably grasp the sensitivity required to work with older people, even or especially with those to whom you are close. Thus, it's important to do the prep work well in advance of talking to any older person. If you feel unsure of how to approach the subject, many wonderful books provide ideas (see the Appendix).

Why can it be so hard to make age-related changes at home? First, most obviously, we're all so darn busy. Second, aging itself may make change more difficult. Ideas get fixed; thinking may be less flexible. Third, change can be expensive, especially on a fixed income. Fourth, our parents' parents died on average younger, quicker and sicker, giving our parents a different model of aging. Fifth, the housing options out there do not always feel acceptable, especially to those who have lived in the family home for decades. Sixth, and finally, adults of all ages feel pressured to stay unrealistically youthful.

That's a lot of reasons! All these factors have resulted in living situations that have not been adapted, that have become counterproductive and sometimes unsafe. As an adult child, you may find it frustrating to see this happen. As an adult getting older yourself, you may wonder how well you'll be able to go with the flow of aging yourself.

If you've (tactfully, yes?) raised the issue of aging at home but run into opposition, how do you respond? Don't nag, and don't become a broken record. Help people think things through. It's hard to change behavior without some insight first, so focus on the thinking. Most people become vaguely aware of a need for change, then actively contemplate a change, then create the conditions for change, then change, then try to maintain the change. Respecting the process, and working with the stage you're at, can increase the odds of success.

Always remember that a change in someone else's home is his or hers to make. You might do well to begin by offering limited choices, not open-ended ideas. Start early so you can slowly work toward agreement. Try to implement changes in a gradual, not abrupt, manner. Remember that one day you too may have the privilege of growing old, and you will want to be treated with the same courtesy and consideration.

In *When Your Loved One Has Alzheimer's: A Caregiver's Guide*, author David L. Carroll offers good advice that works for aging at home in general. Here are his rules of thumb, with the fourth of special import to people sharing a multigenerational home:

1. Adapt the home; don't change it entirely.
2. Simplify the home; don't strip it bare.
3. Modify the environment to the person's particular needs—and do no more.
4. Balance your own needs against those of the elderly or sick person—and strike a happy medium between the two.

Excuses, Excuses: Attitude Adjustment

To take down the attitude barrier to adapting a home for old age, we may have to do some mental "reframing" of the problem. To help, here's some cognitive point-counterpoint: common misconceptions about home modifications and ways to challenge those unhelpful beliefs.

◆ *"It makes me (my mother, father) feel old."* As they do starting in infancy, human needs change and develop over time. This is just the latest phase.

+ *"It will be ugly."* Many helpful items are surprisingly attractive. Redecorating can be unobtrusive and suited to personal taste. In any case, safety and independence really ought to take priority over posh décor.

+ *"I'm fine so far."* Celebrate the situation, then start small to allow people to see that they can live with new approaches. Plan and prepare for incremental change.

+ *"They can't afford it."* Make low-cost fixes first. Even simple changes for common tasks make life better. For example, a reasonably priced grab bar, installed in a couple of hours, can provide a great deal of safety. Also, look into financial aid for seniors through, for example, the local Area Agency on Aging (see the Appendix for additional resources in the United States and Canada).

+ *"We don't know what to do."* Take a class, read brochures and websites, follow the advice in Chapter 8, and acquaint yourself with the resources in the Appendix. Read this book—from start to finish!

+ *"We don't know how to do it."* Do what you can do, then ask people who are handy or hire skilled help to take care of the rest.

+ *"We couldn't sell the house."* Says who? Apply the simple guidelines of Universal Design (read on) and/or make reversible changes. Talk to a local realtor about what does and doesn't sell.

✦ *"They don't own it."* Renting? Borrowing? Make reversible changes, and talk to the landlord: Some permanent changes add value to a property and even make it more desirable to a growing segment of renters—older adults!

Sharing the Care: Geriatric Care Managers

Long- (or short-) distance caregiving? Strapped for time? Consider consulting a geriatric social worker or care manager in the older person's community. Whether a care manager works with a nonprofit or religious agency or independently, this specialized consultant can help solve a myriad of problems by assessing needs, cutting red tape, and potentially recruiting and engaging everyone from drivers to cooks and home health aides (see the Appendix). Sometimes, a third party can even help you find the words to say what needs to be said. And, if you live at a distance, that person can be your local eyes and ears.

Geriatric care managers start an assessment with a phone call or meeting with concerned family members. They should ask what has been going on in the home and what the concerns are. Next comes the home visit. During that time, the care manager will work to establish a relationship, explaining to the clients (the ultimate recipients of their services, regardless of who pays) who they are, what their purpose is, and what they are planning to do.

They might sit with clients and ask what medications they take and when they take them. This provides information about the medical situation and may also expose cognitive issues with reasoning and memory. A trained care manager may also perform what's called a "mini mental" (short for the Mini Mental Status Exam, or MMSE), a brief question-and answer test that may pick up signs of a problem. (Note: The MMSE is no substitute for a proper diagnosis by a family doctor, neurologist or psychiatrist, and is better at tracking changes over time than diagnosing dementia. It's used mostly as a shorthand way to assess problems with memory or orientation.)

Care managers should also ask about interests and hobbies, whether clients have any local support, and if they have financial concerns. They should ask clients how they get around and watch how they walk, get up from a seated position and sit down, and so on.

The next step is a tour of the home (see the checklist, end of this chapter) and an interview with a caregiver, if any. If a client lives alone, a care manager may strongly recommend the installation of a medical alert or emergency response system (see Chapter 7).

Finally, care managers should discuss client eligibility to receive any entitlement benefits. When people have home health policies, the care manager should review these and make sure that they are fully aware of all benefits to which they are entitled.

Open Line: Talking About Aging

Adults caring for elderly parents, relatives and friends find that strong relationships and open communication, if fostered earlier in life, can carry them through the turbulence of later years. However, disease and disability can take a toll on relationships. Pain makes people crabby, cognitive changes can make people mulish. It's also emotionally painful to see once-competent people grow so dependent. Still, you can take three crucial steps without so much as screwing a bolt into the framing of the shower stall.

First, *talk about aging at home, casually, tactfully and regularly*, though not in every conversation—don't be a pest! The discussion should *start* with aging in place, not jump automatically to age-segregated, assisted or institutional living. It's quite possible to age at home, if properly set up. It's like talking to kids about sex: Talk early and talk often. Things will change. Keep asking: "How's it going these days?" A special checklist at the end of this chapter will help you spot the warning signs that something needs to change.

Second, *research the options for aging at home well in advance*: services for aging in place; styles, locations, costs, requirements for admission to other communities. Make a file and update it regularly; new options will appear over time. Learn about local government agencies and nonprofits that help with anything from cleaning to cooking to cabs. Look up and visit the local senior center; learn about clubs, classes and services offered by their faith group or cultural hub, even the local mall. When things are stable and tranquil, that is precious time for preparation. Use it.

Avoid assumptions. Don't rely on hearsay, though you're going to hear plenty. It may go something like this: "*Mrs. Caviar's son found someone to stay with her, sleep on a cot in the attic, bake fresh rolls before dawn, make*

Lobster Thermidor for lunch, give her insulin shots, scrub the toilets, paint the siding, and drive her around in a Lincoln Continental—for $25 a day!" Research the true costs of the various alternatives. The sale of a longtime home might yield enough cash to purchase a more convenient condo. Or, as many people find, it may be less expensive to stay home, set up a caregiver in a spare bedroom, and hire more help for maintenance and renovations. Then again, to some people, hiring and supervising workers and living through the upgrades isn't worth the hassle.

Third, *learn how state or provincial laws define and determine competence and guardianship.* Clearly there are challenges to aging at home—as you've no doubt noticed. Anyone dealing with independent older adults is going to face times of frustration, as well as ethical dilemmas that are fairly new in our society. How do you know when to step in or pull back?

Questions of insight and competence may come up, especially in cases of dementia (progressive cognitive impairment, such as Alzheimer's disease). Although most of us are naturally reluctant to explore these difficult topics, the realities of aging can bring them into play—at times rather quickly.

Should you have any questions, consult an elder-care attorney about whether there are grounds for guardianship, especially if you think people present a danger to themselves or others.

The legal bar for self-determination is high. In layperson terms, you can't just waltz in and change another person's living situation without medical and legal justification, and/or without permission as long as he or she can give it.

More superficially, the same can be said for rearranging the furniture, so hands off without permission. Here's why: Just as they did in their prime, mentally healthy older people weigh their risks against their capabilities. And, just as they did when they were younger, some of them get it right, and some of them get it wrong. The risks are theirs to take, even when it gives the people around them headaches, heartburn or heartache.

Serious misjudgment of risk, such as smoking in bed or climbing a ladder with diabetic foot neuropathy (lack of sensation)—basically, anything endangering themselves or others—calls for outside intervention.

However, should people want to organize their belongings in a way that appears unsightly or inconvenient, that is their right *as long as it is not dangerous.* And should people want to stay at home as long as possible rather than enter "senior housing," that's their right, too. Our job is to help people meet their goals. My job is to help you do that.

The trick is to persuade rather than to force. The task is to encourage and not to dictate. It's best to start small and subtle, not to go for a big dramatic reveal like in a televised home makeover. In short, when you're dealing with someone who is not quite ready for a change, take it a step at a time.

✦ *See her struggling with a jar?* Next week, bring a jar-opening device—and stay for a meal. Ask about arthritis. Learn about her medicines. Talk about exercises that strengthen the hands. Bring a rubber ball to squeeze, and demonstrate how to hold it for 10 seconds, relax for 10 seconds and repeat.

✦ *Learn that he slipped on the stairs?* Take him shopping for new house shoes, closed with rubber soles (and buy yourself a matching pair). Write down his shoe size and ask if you can pick something up. And while you're there, go up and down all the stairs in the house and note the need for any changes (see Chapter 2). Talk about what you have in mind, and of course, find out if any underlying physical or medical change led to the slip.

✦ *Hear them getting depressed about aging?* Commiserate. It truly isn't easy. Then assess whether health changes may be involved, including the onset of clinical depression itself (this calls for professional help). Drop off pictures of attractive rooms designed for age and disability. Find a catalog or website. (Resources are listed in the Appendix). Share this book. Show them examples on the Web, on your laptop or tablet. Tell them what other folks are doing. Give them time to think about their needs.

Safe House: Reducing the Risks

Homes that are safe and functional enable better health and broader ability. As a result, without wanting to scare you, I urge you to think about safety because safe homes raise the odds of being not only safer but more comfortable as well.

Safety and good health often come down to careful management of risk factors and hazards. Huh? What's the difference?

Not to put too fine a point on it, but a *risk factor* is more of an individual condition or circumstance that puts someone at higher risk of having a problem in the future. For example, poor balance makes someone more likely to fall. Low calcium and vitamin D predispose people to osteoporosis.

Hazards tend to be conditions or things in the environment that raise the risk of injury. For example, hazards include shadows on the stairs, stripped electrical wires, unlabeled bottles of bleach, and untended candles or stoves.

Are hazards also risky business? Sure, but the key is to look around and limit them as much as possible.

Some risk factors, such as genetic tendencies, are hard (but not necessarily impossible) to control. Others, such as diet, exercise, sleep, smoking and drug use (often termed "lifestyle" or behavioral factors), can be modified and managed. Hazards, at least in the home (as well as in the workplace and the public arena), can be minimized.

So here's the question. Which is easier: going back in time to drink more milk, or getting rid of throw rugs today? It might be a bit late to meaningfully reduce the odds of a fall-related *fracture*, but reducing the odds of a fall in the first place makes fractures less of a worry.

That's the thinking behind this book. It is meant to help you to spot, remove or correct environmental hazards.

Active Living: ADLs and IADLs

Now that you've embraced your inner Safety Monitor, it's time to meet another big player in aging at home: Activity. *Activity* is simply what we do. Although nowadays the phrase "active living" is used to neutralize negative images of old age—linking it instead to good health and vitality (often! with! exclamation! marks!)—it's also a marketing tool. *"Stewed prunes . . . for your active lifestyle!"*

The truth is that we're active at any age. Even if we're napping at noon or rocking on the porch, that's active, just active at a lower level. It may be more helpful to look at the *kinds* of activities we undertake and, more important, the activities we *want* to undertake, for as long as we can and as well as we can.

Thus, health professionals have developed a common language for understanding any given person's level and type of activity. Allow me to acquaint you with some interesting initials, the ADLs and the IADLs.

Activities of Daily Living (ADLs) are simple. Barring problems, most everyone does these: eating, dressing, bathing and using the toilet. Mild problems with vision, arthritis or mobility can make any of these essential activities harder. Smart kitchen and bathroom tools and thoughtful design can make a big difference.

Of greater complexity, *Instrumental Activities of Daily Living (IADLs)* address the business of living. IADLs include tasks such as shopping, paying the bills, using the phone and cleaning the house. Again, trouble with vision, fine motor problems, and problems with speech, cognition or movement can stand in the way. Mental changes, such as memory loss, often announce themselves first in the IADLs. Adult children find out their parents haven't paid the bills or balanced the checkbook, or a mom who for 30 years has hosted Thanksgiving dinner suddenly finds it overwhelming.

Whether it's with ADLs or IADLs, people like activity. To the best of their abilities, they want to wash, feed and dress themselves; buy their own clothes; clean their closets; and take care of the full range of personal business. A supportive environment can go a long way toward making this possible. Sometimes, something as simple as a high-backed chair in the bedroom and a long-handled shoehorn can help an otherwise able person get dressed. A raised toilet seat (oh, pardon me . . . "comfort height") is essential for bad knees or after hip replacement. Proper lighting in the kitchen will aid cooks in general, and single-lever faucets will help cooks with arthritis in their hands.

These are only some examples of ways to improve the fit between the person and the environment, called, in high-precision scientific jargon, the "person-environment fit." Good fit helps people thrive; poor fit doesn't jive. Good fit for someone with knee problems: a one-level house. Bad fit for someone in a wheelchair: narrow three-level brownstone. Good fit for people using canes: smooth pavement. Bad fit: cobblestones.

You have the general idea. Anything that reduces the demands of the environment will automatically increase ability and allow for more activity of all types and levels. It's like a see-saw, or teeter-totter; as one side goes up, the other goes down. Studying the home for its person-environment fit can also throw a spotlight on risk factors and potential hazards. You know the drill: "An ounce of prevention . . ."

The beauty of person-environment fit is twofold. First, it doesn't blame either a person or a home for being themselves. Second, just like people, it can change over time. Thus, it's recommended that, at any age, people take a good, honest look at their current needs and living situation. Odds are there will be gaps. Closing those gaps is going to help.

How do you do it? That's the easy part! Once people come to terms with the need for a change and inform themselves about their options, action is possible and likely to succeed. The bottom line in home safety for residents of any age comes down to two simple steps:

+ **Step 1: Get rid of as many hazards as possible.** Prevent falls. Prevent fires.
+ **Step 2: Make it easier to get around and do things.** This also boosts safety. For example, using a knife that is easier to grip also lowers the odds of the knife slipping and causing an accidental cut.

Follow these two steps using your own powers of observation, common sense, and the tips and tools in this book. You can also contact an occupational therapist to conduct a more personalized home assessment and make recommendations (see the Appendix).

From this point forward, beyond hazard reduction, your primary guidance will come from an approach to the "built environment" called *Universal Design*.

Easy Does It: Universal Design

Universal Design aims to address the needs of the population as a whole by creating a less restrictive built environment. The goal is to help all people navigate, manipulate and appreciate our world, regardless of age, stage or ability. Rather than offering one solution for disability and another for ability, it strives to offer one good solution for both.

For example, take ramps. Some walkers can go up the stairs, but all walkers can go up a ramp. Therefore, ramps are more universal.

Universal Design solves problems through systematic attention to what exactly happens as we use our world. How do we flush a toilet? How do we open the fridge? Success is measured in terms of accessibility and accommodation, depending on the need.

Accessibility makes it easier to get in and out of a room, a house, a store, a stadium. Breaking down all-too-common barriers to access, it means adding ramps to buildings that only had stairs, putting Braille and beepers into elevators, making cuts in raised curbs (good for strollers, bikes, shopping carts, wheeled luggage *and* wheelchairs), creating safe walkways through parking lots, widening doors to toilet stalls, laying down nonslip flooring, improving transitions from nonskid tile to carpets or wood floors, and installing big, round and obvious buttons at wheelchair height to open doors.

In the home, accessibility might mean having pocket doors that slide into the walls, replacing swinging doors that guzzle space. Or it might mean installing a roll-in shower, an entrance ramp, wider hallways or an automated stair lift. Accessibility opens more living space and allows for safe, smooth passage inside and out.

Accommodation, on the other hand, makes it easier to manage with a physical or mental limitation, for example through tools or technologies that compensate for fading powers. Eyeglasses are a classic accommodation. Hearing aids are another. So are canes, wheelchairs, scooters, long-handled shoehorns (you mean you don't have one?), motorized windows, gripping devices to help open jars, pill-minder gadgets, grab bars, electric can openers, fat rubberized pens, big-button phones, and a vast and growing array of devices invented solely for our comfort and pleasure. Even shopping lists and address books are assistive technologies: They accommodate limited memory.

To be truly universal, product or space design should meet the following criteria, according to The Center for Universal Design at North Carolina State University.

- ✦ **Equitable Use:** can be used by people with diverse abilities and address a variety of needs, such as sitting and standing.
- ✦ **Flexibility in Use:** accommodates a wide range of individual preferences and abilities, such as a

trash can in which the lid also opens with a foot pedal, or a gadget that works for both righties and lefties.

✦ **Simple and Intuitive Use:** accommodates different levels of literacy and language skills, experience and knowledge, such as through large and obvious "on/off" controls.

✦ **Perceptible Information:** communicates necessary information effectively regardless of the user's sensory abilities or local conditions; for example, big-button phones and remotes, loud timers.

✦ **Tolerance for Error:** minimizes and warns about hazards and the fallout from accidents; for example, through glare-reducing surfaces and nonslip floors.

✦ **Low Physical Effort:** can be used efficiently and comfortably with less fatigue, such as fat pen barrels or counter-height microwave ovens.

✦ **Size and Space for Approach and Use:** appropriate for reaching, manipulations and use regardless of body size, posture or mobility; for example, wheelchair- and walker-friendly spaces with clear lines of sight to important elements and adequate space for assistive devices or personal assistance.

Making space accessible and accommodating limitations can restore a reasonable amount of freedom and ability to an older person's life. So, as you embark on this journey, look for ways to create access and increase accommodation.

— ◆ —

John and Patricia from our opening story began to boost their staying power by converting a downstairs public room to a bedroom and hiring a gardener for the more demanding outdoor work. It might also be a good time to acquaint themselves with area resources that could help them stay at home longer, such as food delivery and cleaning services. Increasingly, elder-care companies send services into the home. Or if John and Patricia really want out of that house, they can assess their finances and consider smaller, owned or rented housing short of continuing care.

THE 5-SENSE TOUR
Spot the Early Warning Signs of Trouble

How do you know if you or your loved ones need help? Sometimes the signs are obvious and sometimes, not so much. Use all your senses—common sense and the other five—to determine if it's time to intervene. Just remember, if you look around on a visit, please try to be inconspicuous. No one likes a snoop.

Sight
1. Is the house orderly and clean?
2. Is there an unusual amount of mail, garbage, clutter, dust or dirt?
3. In the kitchen, are there dirty dishes in the sink and on the counter? Is food left out? Are there bugs?

4. Are there scorch marks on the pot holders or dish towels? Are there signs that pots burned on the stove?

5. In the bathroom, is the shower curtain torn around any rings, meaning someone may have grabbed it in a fall? Have soap dishes or towel racks come down? Are the bathtub and the shower clean? Are there signs of recent use?

Sound

1. Test the doorbell: Can they hear it? Do you have to ring a lot, and/or knock loudly?

2. Can they easily hear the telephone?

3. Is the telephone programmed to ring enough times (before the answering system starts) to allow them to reach it without rushing?

4. Are emergency numbers programmed into the phones?

5. Do they play the TV, stereo or radio so loud that you can't hold a conversation?

6. If there's an intercom system (useful in a multi-level house), is it in working order?

Smell

1. Does the living environment have any unpleasant odors?

2. Do the refrigerator or cupboards smell?

3. Are towels, linens and clothes closets fresh, and are there signs of recent laundering? Are the soap supplies slowly dwindling through regular use?

4. Is there a mildew smell and/or are there water stains under the sink and in other places, which could result from forgotten running water?

5. Is there a smell of natural gas? Sense of smell diminishes with age, so check this every time. If you smell gas, get everyone to leave immediately and call the gas company from a cell phone or a neighbor's house.

Taste

1. Does the pantry have a variety of freshly stocked items?

2. How does the food taste? Look at the expiration dates.

3. Does the water taste right if it's filtered; are the filters up to date? Do they have a fresh supply?

4. If they use a water softener, is the unit properly filled with salt crystals? Do they have extra (very heavy) bags? Can you arrange for regular delivery?

5. Are stronger seasonings needed to enhance the flavor of foods and make them more palatable?

Touch

1. Do the doors and windows open easily? How about the locks?

2. Is the furniture dusty? The floor sticky and grimy? How about the tub and sinks?

3. Are knives housed in a safe place so no one gets cut by accident?

4. Is it easy to reach glassware and other breakables?
5. Do telephones and appliances have large-type buttons? Are the controls easy to read and use, and are things in good working order?

Adapted with permission from Using Your Five Senses to Assess Your Loved One's Care Needs, *CK Franchising Inc. (www.comfortkeepers.com)*

Chapter 2

The Stable Home: Preventing Falls

Dateline: Tucson. An active woman in her early 60s, Carol was determined to stay fit. Trying a new aerobic exercise routine in her living room, she tripped over the edge of her beautiful heirloom rug, fell to the floor and learned the hard way—the very hard way—that she had osteoporosis. She's one of the lucky ones. One hip replacement and one hip-replacement upgrade later, she's doing well, walks as much as she can and is always looking for new ways to raise her staying power.

— ◆ —

Falls are often named as the No. 1 fear of people getting older for good reason. Authorities cite falls as the leading cause of injury to older people, with fall-related injuries all too often causing their death either at the time or within a year. In addition:

✦ The risk of falls increases with age.
✦ One fall makes more falls increasingly likely.
✦ Falls are the most common cause of traumatic brain injury, which accounts for nearly half the fatalities from adult falls.
✦ People 75 and older who fall are *four to five times more likely* to be admitted to a nursing home for one year or longer.

Falls also create a fear of falls, which leads people to limit what they do. This makes them more housebound, which actually makes it more likely that they'll fall again.

According to the American Geriatrics Society, older persons should be evaluated for risk of falling if they are worried about or frightened by a fall, fell two or more times in the past year, fell one or more times with injury or have problems with balance when walking.

It is abundantly clear that falls are an enormous problem, painful and costly to individuals, loved ones and society. But why do older people fall more often? You name it, they have it:

✦ poor vision
✦ slower reflexes (it's harder to stop a fall)
✦ poor balance, or problems staying upright after losing equilibrium
✦ weak muscles in the upper and lower body
✦ drowsiness or dizziness due to insomnia, low blood pressure or medication

◆ slower walking speed (gait), which might not cause falls directly but reflects all of the above, making it a useful measure.

Falls leave people with everything from bruised egos to sore muscles, broken hips, hospital stays, or lasting disability and dependency. People who "slip and trip" don't think they've fallen, but they might have—and the next time, they might actually go all the way. Bad breaks appear to ultimately shorten lives due to downward spirals in health and activity; really bad falls can be fatal.

That said, are falls an inevitable part of aging? Not necessarily, at least not in the numbers we're seeing and with such dire outcomes. People can build a strong core and lower body, and use that strength to develop balance through recommended exercise programs such as tai chi, recently recommended by the American Geriatrics Society and the British Geriatrics Society. At the same time, try to fall-proof the home environment as much as possible.

Doctors may recommend dietary or supplemental calcium and vitamin D to help strengthen bones. It's also advised to have them review the prescriptions of all older patients for any that might raise the risk of falling, such as antidepressants, anti-anxiety drugs and sleep aids.

Also, do not rush! Rushing is a major cause of falls and—this is a scientifically proven fact, so pay attention—much other needless stupidity.

As a side note, many older individuals are startled when seemingly minor falls break their hips and not their wrists or arms. Why? It's not just osteoporosis. As we get older or more inactive, we stop falling forward on our hands because of weaker reflexes and balance. We fall back and to the side, hitting the hips instead. So there you go.

Pick Up the Pieces: Tripping Hazards

The first step in fall prevention is to remove obvious hazards. These can include anything from electrical, TV and phone cords to computer cables and toys for pets and grandchildren. Tape or tack cords along the wall. Better yet, in the case of lamps, eliminate cords by installing ceiling and wall lighting.

Ensure that someone picks up toys (preferably the toy owner) after every use and stows them in a basket or a laundry tub. Speaking of baskets, they're useful for carrying collections of items while freeing a hand to grip the stair rail. Rubber dishpans and small laundry baskets may also suffice.

Train folks to mop up every spill, even small ones, right away. Become obsessive-compulsive, at least about cleaning the floor.

Next, do boots and shoes have to be scattered across foyer floors like so many land mines waiting to shatter bones? Especially in colder climates, these freeways of footwear are jammed with accidents waiting to happen. You can ask people to leave their shoes out of the traffic flow. You can try to train people of all ages to neatly place their shoes and boots along the wall in pairs. Or you can just steal their shoes.

Human nature being what it is, people still might not get the point. Train the children, hope for the best with the adults, and use environmental cues. Here are some possible solutions:

+ Along the wall, place rubber or plastic trays (boot trays or similar mats) that contrast with the floor, as many as you need with an extra for guests.
+ Leave a bright pair of cute children's shoes there year-round as a playful cue for visitors.
+ Tape or tack a "Put Shoes Here" sign on the wall above the trays, with an arrow pointing down. "Please" is optional.
+ Set up a short plastic rope line behind which shoes are placed.
+ Or, if there's room, set out a plastic hamper or large wicker basket with a tag or sign, "Shoes Go Here."
+ Tape several bright carpet squares along the wall.
+ Provide a basket or dishpan of washable, one-size-fits all rubber-soled house slippers.

Umbrella stands are also useful. To avoid slippery drips, line an attractive wastebasket in plastic. Weigh it down with rocks or a couple of bricks.

Purses, briefcases, laptop cases and shopping bags also need an appointed place—hooks, shelves, a bench or a trunk—to keep them and their nasty straps off the floor.

Finally, as they get older or weaker, many people begin to lean on any available surface for support. Be sure that furniture in the path of walking is sturdy and tall enough to offer support. Low tables are a tripping hazard; take them out of the traffic path. Rocking chairs and gliders may need to be taken out of harm's way. Remove casters from chairs and ottomans. And hem bedding and drapes to make sure they don't trail onto the floor.

Sure Footing: Flooring

With age, it gets harder to see the floor, for feet to sense changes in flooring levels and surfaces, and to correct for changes in position. Thus, your task is to create as smooth and continuous a surface as possible.

The first step is to remove anything that can cause people to trip, such as small throw or scatter rugs. Even when taped, their edges ride up. Even with nonslip backing, they can move. Some have old-fashioned fringe as well. Can it be removed? Securely tape area rugs and lay them over nonslip pads. Repair any rips or holes.

Of course, it would be best if you got rid of them altogether, so indulge me for a minute as I holler: *Death to Scatter Rugs!*

Burn them. Shred them. Turn them into wall hangings or place mats. Sell them on Craigslist or eBay. Stimulate the economy. Just take them off the floor. To paraphrase one of my professors, who was hectoring us in another context: *Yes, you can keep your scatter rugs if you want, and yes, you can even tape the edges.* **But only if you want to fall.**

I'll shut up now.

Meanwhile, wall-to-wall carpet (or broadloom) isn't necessarily the answer. Some people who walk with difficulty find it takes more energy to move across a thick pile carpet. On stairs, carpeting can wear down and become slippery (we'll talk more about stairs later in this chapter). Some people install industrial- or commercial-type carpets. These are practical and lower maintenance than cut-pile carpets and offer some surprisingly attractive styles and colors. As a bonus, they can also be cleaned with much lighter-weight vacuums.

Then there's tile. Not only is it hard, but it is slippery when wet. Homeowners who want floor tile for its looks or ease of maintenance can still make it more user-friendly. First, install the right kind of tile, with a little texture and greater slip resistance. It will look more matte and less shiny. Ask the dealer to look up a tile's "coefficient of friction," or how hard it pushes back against another surface, such as your foot, for use in wet areas such as kitchens and bathrooms.

In some cases, you may have to push a little, or find another dealer. Salespeople who have never heard of the coefficient of friction (COF) or who stroke the tile and say things like, "This feels really nice" are not helpful. Or it could be that the store offers a line of tile that hasn't been systematically graded.

According to the Ceramic Tile Institute, slip-resistant tile has a friction coefficient of 0.60 or greater (wet). This tile meets or exceeds general safety and health regulations, as well as the requirements of the Americans With Disabilities Act (ADA) and the Occupational Health and Safety Administration (OSHA). Conditionally Slip Resistant tile is rated at 0.50 to 0.59 (wet), which meets or exceeds general safety and health regulations and OSHA requirements, but not those of the ADA. In other words, they're adequate for able-bodied workers wearing appropriate garb but not for individuals with impaired gait or balance, or who are frail. Tiles with a friction coefficient of less than 0.50 have questionable slip resistance.

Second, consider using smaller tiles. Smaller tiles require more grout lines, creating an attractive design that increases friction and reduces slippery surface area. More slip-resistant tiles, set in more grout, are also less shiny, and less likely to reflect light and create the kind of glare that bothers older eyes.

As for wood floors, they're warmer and more resilient than tile, have a little "give," and look great. However, the glare of high-gloss finishes is very hard on older eyes. Whether you refinish or install new wood or laminate floors, select a satin or low-luster finish. Bright and shiny objects are kid stuff.

For tub and shower floors, put down nonslip tub decals or nonslip waterproof mats. Check quality and durability, which vary widely. To cover the entire tub floor, you can cut up an additional mat. For mats with suction cups, check every so often to ensure that the cups really, you know, suck. For regular bathroom floors, use rubber-bottomed bath mats.

Floor and door sills, or thresholds, are another potential tripping hazard. If the transitions from the outside to inside, or from room to room, are lumpy and bumpy, speak with a contractor about ways to smooth them out through beveled edges, broader cover plates or other options. Please, the author says wearily, do not throw yet another rug or mat over the threshold to "smooth it out." That's just asking for trouble.

Look Around: Layout and Lighting

Next on the fall-prevention menu: How are things laid out in the home? Does the décor provide adequate lighting?

Here's why we ask. By the time we're 50, we need about three times as much light to see as we did when we were 20. Our eyes must work harder to do the same tasks.

Brighter light bulbs alone won't help. They may overload the fixtures, add too much heat, use too much energy, and create unwanted glare. (So first make sure your parents' lamps aren't packing more wattage than they're supposed to carry. Cross reference fire prevention.) Compact fluorescents can give greater candlepower without these drawbacks. In overhead fixtures, they last a long time if left on. That means fewer bulb changes, itself a safety measure.

If it's possible to make bigger adjustments, consider adding more overhead lighting, which is even and can cover more areas of the room. Overhead lighting eliminates shadows and dark areas, such as the turn in a staircase, room corners, or anywhere people make a transition, such as a threshold between rooms. Just one or two fixtures might do the trick. Lighting that can be adjusted by dimmer switches can be even more useful.

After overhead lighting, the next best type is wall-mounted lighting, such as electrical sconces. Even as vision dims, beware of adding table and floor lamps. Not only does that create more hard-to-process islands of light and dark, but it adds trip-and-slip inducing lamp cords.

Dimmers allow us to make almost any light source more pleasing and comfortable. Dimmable fluorescent bulbs are starting to come on the market but require a dimmer switch that works with their much lower wattage. Other lighting technologies are emerging, such as energy-efficient light-emitting diodes (LEDs) grouped into screw-in bulbs that handle being cycled on and off better than fluorescents. LEDs are also used for innovative rope-lighting applications, running around ceilings, down stairwells and more.

Nightlights are an obvious boon, especially to people who get up at night to use the bathroom. Again, these vary. Some have a soft glow; others are bright. Most people know what light level is enough to guide them when they're up, without disturbing their ability to go back to sleep. Again, older eyes need more light. Illuminated light switches are also useful, though not strong enough to light the floor and thresholds.

Motion-activated lights that come on automatically are especially useful at night when people are groggy.

Going Up! Stairs and Stair Rails

Stairs are to aging as pimples are to teenagers: Most of us get them, and we don't know how to make them go away. Together with bathrooms, stairs account for more injuries than any other part of the house. Yet even in a home where stairs and rails are poorly equipped or proportioned, you can take steps (*get it? steps?*) to improve comfort and safety going up and down.

First and foremost, always wear securely fastened shoes or slippers that aren't slippery, most obviously with rubber soles.

Second, the American Geriatrics Society has issued a caution about bifocal or multifocal lenses. Looking down into the near-vision part of the lens makes it hard to judge depth and see obstacles. On the stairs, wearers should use the handrail and take off the glasses during the transition if that helps them feel more comfortable. Multifocal lenses may be tricky during some outdoor activities as well.

One practical solution could be to look out the upper (not for reading) portion of eyeglasses while always using stair handrails and compensating in other ways. People depend on their glasses for different needs, and those who don't need them for everything might gain flexibility and free their hands through the use of an eyeglasses chain, pocket, fanny pack or lightweight bag for glasses. Reading glasses can be kept near a reading chair or bed. In any case, counsel the bespectacled to mind their vision when they go downstairs.

Third, let's look at stairs themselves. Disability guidelines mandate that treads, the part you step on, be at least 11 inches deep. Stair risers, which are the vertical part you kick if the tread is too shallow, should measure 4 to 7 inches high. (Shorter rises are easier for people with decreased strength, mobility or endurance.) If you see scuff marks, either your feet are too big or your tread is too shallow. Stair width should be at least 36 inches. Open treads, without sealed risers, are dangerous and taboo.

Building codes give looser parameters. Case in point: The stair risers in my 1977 house are adequate, but the treads, at about 9 inches, are not. We have to point our feet in or out to fit the treads, which alters body alignment and doesn't feel very secure.

Repair or replace worn-out treads, but otherwise, short of ripping out and rebuilding the stairs, it's hard to change their dimensions. Thus, if your stairs fall short (so to speak), focus on other aspects of the scenario.

Stair rails are essential. It's best to have them on two sides to allow for the use of either or both hands, depending on comfort and ability. If one side of the body is disabled, temporarily or permanently, someone can at least use the stronger and more able side. Handrails are generally mounted from 36 to 39 inches from the floor, with an inch and a half of clearance from the wall. Bolt them to the wall studs. Just as with grab bars, there's no point in falling and ripping out a chunk of wall as you go down.

Safety councils specify standards for handrails, so if you're interested in this level of detail, find them on the Internet. Suffice it to say that a standard, traditional, hand-sized rounded handrail with a grooved grasping area for fingers works best. Most are flat-bottomed for easier installation. Decorative rails, such as modern squared-off wood or decorative wrought iron, are harder to grip in the case of a fall or loss of balance.

Regardless of the type of stairs you have, there's plenty you can do.

Start with lighting. To illuminate a stairway for the entire trip up and down, an electrician can install three-way switches that work at both the top and bottom of each staircase. (Surprisingly, not all homes have these switches, which work equally well for long hallways.) For stairs that turn, wall- or ceiling-mounted spotlights with two or three flexible heads can shed extra light on the shadows that haunt corners and endanger people who are, when you think about it, off balance and turning while simultaneously loosening their grip on a handrail, or changing from one rail to another.

Additionally, a new idea is to tack rope lights, tiny lights encased in clear tubing (often used for holidays), along the side walls of stair treads and risers.

Next, go to work on the stairs. First make sure the handrails contrast with the walls, making them easier to see. Paint, stain or wrap-around friction tape can help (the tape also makes the grip more secure).

Safety experts also recommend good contrast between the last step and the landing, which are often the same color. You can achieve the color change by tacking to the landing a sturdy rubber floor mat in a different color.

Some people paint contrasting stripes to edge the stairs. But while these call attention to the edges of the steps, they don't offer slip resistance.

Instead, lay down two or three strips of traction tape that contrast with the stair color across the front of every smooth-surfaced stair tread (obviously, this won't work on carpet). Covered in grit like a nail file or sandpaper, traction tape or safety treads (found in hardware stores) help in two ways.

First, contrasting tape gives those going down a visual cue as to where treads ends. That's an important, underestimated fix. Second, the friction serves to slow everyone down. It doesn't look as bad as you might think, and it won't permanently damage floors. (Though, you know, sometimes you have to weigh the expense of damaged wood against the cost of a damaged person.)

If you can repair the wood later or leave as is, nail or glue down commercial-grade rubber safety treads. Commercial safety products in general offer ideas that might be useful around the house.

It's important to have the railings begin and end at a convenient position for grasping so no one has to lean forward to get the railing. So, if possible, extend handrails by a few inches at the top and bottom of the stairs. At the top, the extension will help people get a good grip before stepping off balance. At the bottom (or landing), people can steady themselves as their momentum shifts. And stair rails should return to the wall rather than stay open so that sleeves don't catch on them.

The newel or center post of a staircase should be topped with a sturdy finial to serve as a kind of hand brake.

Does it need to be said that stairs should be kept clear? Items to go up and down can be placed near the top or bottom of the stairs out of the direct pathway, perhaps in wicker baskets with tall handles. Load them up throughout the day to save unnecessary trips. Know anyone handy? Improvise a rope-and-pulley system. Old-fashioned dumbwaiters were smart.

In terms of behavior, the main thing for stair climbers is to be aware of and adjust to changing heights. That means slowing down. As has been sarcastically observed, so many accidents come from needless rushing.

Finally, muscle strength and flexibility can turn the use of stairs from an exhausting chore into something approximating weight-bearing exercise—your own personal, low-cost stair climbing machine. People shouldn't have to feel as if they're pulling themselves up Mount Everest. Strong leg, hip and bottom muscles make it easier to push off and land. In fact, did you know going down works the muscles surrounding the knee joint harder than going up? Core strength makes it easier to stay upright, especially as we turn. And upper-body strength helps us make the best use of the rails, to pace ourselves safely, and correct for dips and slips. (Read more about at-home fitness in Chapter 6.)

For folks whose stair-climbing days are done, or temporarily interrupted by injury or illness, learn about automated chairlifts in Chapter 4.

Finally, although step stools are available, it is far safer to avoid their use. Place much-used items at a lower level. Don't step up to retrieve them, especially if there are problems with balance or dizziness. Never, ever climb on chairs or other unstable surfaces.

Sinking Feeling: Sunken Rooms

Sunken rooms pose a hazard to older people in particular. It would be hard to have any kind of ramp to correct for the step, but residents who are stuck in this situation can try other safety measures.

Consider installing handrails or grab bars to a side or entry wall. It would also help to install overhead lighting and mark the edge of the upper level all around, perhaps with no-slip or traction tape in a contrasting color. Forget carpeting over the edge of the step, as this can get worn, stretched out and slippery.

Another option: If the ceiling is high enough and the area small enough, you could consider filling in the sunken area and leveling out the floor. However, if you've reached that level of concern, it might be time for bigger changes.

Belly Up to the Grab Bar

Though we don't think of them that way, stair rails are simply specialized grab bars. Maybe we don't think of them in that respect because grab bars are a visible sign of disability, the first thing people think of when they hear "accommodation." That makes most of us uncomfortable. Grab bars speak to us of old age, crippling arthritis, nasty falls and hospital rooms. Ugh. We'd rather think we'll never fall. Nope. Not us.

Until we do, and then it's *all* we think about.

So before you say no to grab bars—*no, not that, anything but that*—let's talk. Think of other instances when you changed your mind about something that, at the time, seemed inconceivable.

Think about, say, recessed or pot lights. When they came in, they seemed ugly and distracting. Then we got used to them. They came to seem elegant. They even provided dimmable light we could control from the wall. They helped us to get rid of evil lamp cords.

Now, we have to get used to something new again, something with at least as much potential to help us live better. All of us, young and old, will learn to view grab bars as friends who come in peace. And they're especially essential in the bathroom, where people often fall given the wet and slippery conditions. But there will be a period of adjustment.

To help, home-health product designers are stepping up with increasingly attractive offerings. Contractors are learning how to install grab bars properly (to the studs, or it *hikes* the danger). And we will adapt, because adaptation makes a species successful.

Here are some places where grab bars are useful:

1. The bathtub and shower—both inside, and going in and out
2. Next to the toilet, for getting on and off
3. Next to the bed, for getting in and out
4. Next to a favorite reading/TV chair
5. At the top and bottom of a staircase
6. In sunken living rooms or bedrooms.

© iStockphoto.com/nazdravie

The photo above shows an example of the different ways that grab bars can be used in a traditional bathtub installation.

Now for the technical part: Select grab bars with textured, slip-resistant grips, with a rough or a diamond (peened) finish, that feel right to the hands. These are especially important in the tub, where hands and bars will be soapy and wet. Diameters vary; some older adults with arthritis prefer the smaller sizes. Longer grab bars provide—naturally—more area to grab. It may be tempting to buy grab bars that blend with the décor, but bars that blend are hard to see. Bright colors stand out and look more decorative than stainless steel.

Tub- and suction-mounted bars are not recommended.

They are often installed incorrectly and are not up for the job. By giving the bather a false sense of security, they may actually increase risk.

If the hardware or home-health store offers a limited variety of grab bars, ask to see a catalog. Use the offerings in stock to get a general idea of what you and your folks want, then go online for better-stocked suppliers (see the Appendix).

Here are additional things to know about grab bars, adapted with permission from guidelines provided by Weill Cornell Medical College's Program in Environmental Geriatrics:

Before purchasing a wall-mounted grab bar, ask:

✦ Is the bar long enough to be accessed from several locations while sitting and standing?

✦ Does the diameter fit the user's grip? A large person will need a bigger diameter than a frail older person with arthritic hands.

✦ Is the bar textured enough to keep wet hands from slipping but not too rough for fragile skin? Many people like a brushed (peened) or a rippled (diamond) finish. Texture is especially important for vertically mounted grab bars.

✦ Have you chosen a bright color to contrast with the surroundings? These are easier to see and less industrial looking than stainless steel.

✦ Is the bar able to sustain 250 pounds of—egads—dead-load force?

Before installing a grab bar, know:

+ Wall surface: Is it in good condition? If the tiles are bulging or cracked, repair the wall before installing grab bars.
+ Wall composition: Knowing whether the wall is concrete, tile with plaster board, masonry, etc., allows the installer to choose the appropriate fastener.
+ Water pipe location: Smart contractors will ask the owner or landlord for their location. Accidentally drilling into a water pipe can cause extensive damage.
+ If the installer has experience installing grab bars.
+ If the installation method is strong enough to support someone's weight during a fall (there's that dead-load force—greater than weight alone, thanks to momentum!).
+ If grab bars will be bolted securely to the wall studs; drywall plugs are not enough.
+ If there are no studs, or there are studs in the wrong places: Install grab bars into plywood blocking or cross braces spiked between the studs.
+ To use a diamond-tipped drill to bore neat holes through ceramic tiles.
+ That fasteners must also meet code.

Grab 'n' Go: Bathroom Safety

Determine grab bar location by holding a fully clothed "dress rehearsal," getting in and out of a dry shower or bathtub. Mark the locations where users have a safe and comfortable reach. Horizontal bars mounted about 33 to 36 inches high (more for tall folks) are useful on the shorter side wall to help people get in and out of the tub. For people who prefer a vertical bar there, install it no more than 9 inches from the edge of the outside tub wall, with the bottom nearly 3 feet from the floor.

A long bar along the long wall makes a great hand grip for standing or using a bath chair. If mounted lower, some 9 to 11 inches above the rim of the tub, it can help people pull up from the tub floor, transfer in and out of a wheelchair, and go from seated to standing when using a bath chair.

The use of angled bars may seem like a useful compromise, but it is controversial because wet hands can slide down them easily and they can be harder to grasp during a fall.

In related washroom news, roll-in showers are becoming more popular, allowing users to avoid climbing over the porcelain lip of a tub or the metal floor rails of a stand-alone shower. In these showers, the floor slants toward the drain. Shower curtains or accordion-style doors provide easier access.

In the absence of a roll-in shower, a special seat called a transfer bench allows people to more easily enter and leave the tub. In the case of injury or disability, physical and occupational therapists will demonstrate the use of this simple but crucial piece of equipment. Read more about bathroom safety in Chapter 4.

Is there a nightlight in the bathroom, and is the door left open at bedtime?

Finally, toilet safety rails come in many shapes and sizes, the common denominator being that they help people get on and off the toilet. And while you're at it, see if it's easy to reach the toilet paper from the seated position. See? We think of everything.

Now is the time to get off the commode and take command of fall prevention. Remember Carol in Tucson with her osteoporosis and a new hip? She maximized her staying power by selling that rug on Craigslist and using the money to treat her family to a weekend away . . . and installing two grab bars in the bathtub.

LET'S GET STARTED
Top Tips for a Stable Home

___ Ensure the use of proper footwear.

___ Discuss the proper wearing of multifocal glasses.

___ Remove tripping hazards.

___ Supply paper towels in kitchen to wipe floor spills immediately.

___ Assess use and function of step stools and ladders.

___ Remove furniture casters.

___ Remove scatter rugs.

___ Tape area rugs securely.

___ Ensure "pathway" furniture is strong and stable.

___ Provide nonslip mats, transfer benches, tub seats and grab bars in bathroom.

___ Install grab bars outside washroom as needed.

___ Assess and update lighting.

___ Assess existing flooring and thresholds.

☑ LET'S GO SHOPPING
Top Tools for a Stable Home

☐ Rubber-soled shoes and slippers

☐ Reading-glass holders

☐ Fanny packs/light bags to carry multifocal glasses

☐ Wall tape and/or tacks for power and computer cords

☐ Woven and laundry baskets or dish tubs for items to go up or down stairs

☐ Rubber/plastic boot trays (color contrast with the floor)

☐ Stands and plastic rope for shoe rope line

☐ Carpet squares

☐ Guest house slippers with nonslip soles

☐ Umbrella stand: new wastebasket with plastic lining, weighted

☐ Front hall/foyer storage to keep parcels and purses off the floor

☐ Nonslip tub and bathroom mats

☐ Compact fluorescent/LED bulbs

☐ Grab bars galore!

☐ Friction tape (usually black but also comes in white for the bathtub/shower)

☐ Tub transfer bench, tub seat, handheld showerhead

Chapter 3

The Smoke-Free Home: Preventing Fires

Betty loved to cook. She cooked well, she cooked often, and she cooked for everybody—the son she lived with, his wife, their daughters and the daughters' friends and boyfriends in their big St. Louis house. Physically, she seemed to have a lot of staying power, but a worry was slowly creeping into the kitchen: Betty was getting forgetful. Increasingly often, her family would come home to find a neglected pot burning on the stove, a dried-out roast in a hot oven, an empty kettle that was all whistled out. Betty didn't seem to notice—and no one wanted to hurt her feelings (or go hungry).

— ✦ —

If you thought that falls were a hot topic, wait till you hear about fires. Often underestimated as a source of danger for older people, fires are actually the No. 2 safety concern. For people age 65 and older, the risk of dying in a fire is three times greater than it is for younger people. Fires can cause everything from smoke inhalation and permanent lung damage to life-threatening burns. And, of course, they also damage property.

The primary fire hazards are as follows: kitchen fires (kitchen grease or toaster crumbs; hair and clothing catching fire); faulty electrical wiring, heaters and appliances; and smoking, including falling asleep with a lit cigarette.

Although fires are a risk for people of any age, the normal changes of aging can raise the risk by making it harder to see hazards, smell smoke or leaking gas, and remember something's on the stove. Older people are less able to take quick action, sometimes due to medication. In addition, they may be more vulnerable because they often live alone.

Slow Burn: Reduce the Risk of Fire

Fire prevention calls for simple common sense.

First, go through the home and take stock of all flammable materials, such as cleaners and paint thinners. Label them clearly (especially important for people with poor vision) and store them properly, away from sources of heat and flame.

Second, post the emergency-number 911 in the kitchen, at bedside, and next to every other phone in the house. If there's a separate number for the local fire department, post that along with your clearly lettered street address. In an emergency, some people may panic and forget where they live. Some fire departments may be able to send someone to inspect the premises for potential hazards. If so, invite them over. You can also let the local police and fire departments know that you or your older parents live alone.

Third, install smoke alarms on every story of the home (not too close to cooking areas) and outside sleeping areas. Fire safety experts also recommend installing a smoke alarm inside each bedroom. If nuisance alarms— when cooking or using the shower—are a problem, install smoke alarms with a "hush" feature. These devices have a button that will temporarily silence the alarm for 7 to 10 minutes before they automatically reset.

Test all smoke alarms regularly and replace the batteries once a year or when the low-battery warning chirps. To avoid climbing on a chair or step stool, test the alarms by gently pressing the test buttons with a broom handle or cane tip.

Consider installing wireless, interconnected smoke alarms, so that when one alarm is triggered, they all sound. Information about fire safety for the deaf or hard of hearing is available from the U.S. Fire Administration (see the Appendix). Visual alarms with strobe lights, on every level of the home, are a must in this situation.

Escape Hatch: Plan Your Exit

Develop a home fire-escape plan and practice it with everyone in the household. Make sure everyone knows two ways out of each room, if possible. Check that all exits are unobstructed and easy to use. Determine who will be responsible for helping anyone who may need assistance. Choose a meeting place outside where you can account for everyone.

If caught in smoke, get low and go under the smoke to the nearest safe exit. Call the fire department from outside the home. Once out, stay out. Never re-enter a burning building.

Now let's smoke out some additional fire-prevention tips.

Flash in the Pan: Cooking Fires

We'll start with the obvious. To keep hair and clothes away from flames, make sure cooks of any age keep their hair regularly trimmed and, if necessary, tied back. Maybe stash a few hair ties and clips in a cup near the stove. Urge cooks not to work in a bathrobe or anything with flowing sleeves. They should also turn pot handles in to avoid knocking them off the stove, and whenever possible, use only the rear burners. If clothing catches fire, *stop, drop* to the ground, and *roll* over and over to smother the flames.

Next, get a loud kitchen timer, even if the cook plans to remain in the kitchen. Cooking should never be left unattended. How many times do people put something up and plan to stay around, only to be distracted by the doorbell, a phone call, or someone wanting their attention? Modern digital beep-beep timers might not be sufficiently loud; test a timer in the store if you can. Is it screechy and annoying? Buy it!

Check to see whether the "on" and "off" positions of stove dials are clearly marked. Organizations for people with visual limitations (see Appendix for further resources) offer tools for marking stove dials in bright colors. Informed cooks can set proper heat levels. Newer appliances place controls at the front of the stove, which is a safer place for all ages to use.

Electric kettles might be another good option because they shut off automatically after water comes to a boil.

Cooking habits may need to change. It makes sense to cook more often in a microwave oven, especially at counter height and not overhead. Deep frying is not only a fire hazard but its oxidized fat content isn't good for us. Greater care with the use of oils generally is called for; nonstick pans can help, along with cooking in broth.

If a fire starts in a pot, put on a heat-proof oven glove and then slide a proper-fitting lid over the pot to smother the flames. Turn off the burner when it is safe to do so. *Do not* use water to extinguish a stovetop fire, or attempt to move the burning pot to the sink or outside.

To combat fire inside a toaster oven, close the door to deprive the fire of oxygen and unplug the appliance. *Again: Never put water on a cooking fire!*

To prevent fire-prone buildup, be sure the oven and stove are clean. Clean out toaster and toaster-oven crumbs weekly or more often. Regular cleaning of cooking equipment reduces hazardous buildup of crumbs and flammable grease. Mark regular cleaning sessions on a separate calendar kept to track monthly and annual household chores.

When shopping for a new stove, bear in mind that a smooth-top surface is safer than something with open flames. Barbecues are for outdoor use only. Never bring propane barbecue tanks inside the home.

Fire safety experts recommend that if you can't contain a small blaze, get out and stay out. Call the fire department once safely outside.

The use of home fire extinguishers is not generally recommended for older people, who may have slower reaction times and mobility issues. Extinguishers are fine for trained users, but most people are not trained—and a fire is not the time to fumble with the manual.

Given how quickly fire spreads and the way it can harm your health, especially with the toxic and combustible materials in recent homes, in most cases the best thing to do is get out and leave the firefighting to the pros.

Live Wires: Prevent Electrical Fires

Especially for older or renovated homes, it's well worth the minor expense to hire a licensed electrician to check the wiring and circuits or fuses. It is also wise to replace outdated fuses with dedicated circuit breakers.

Check room by room for wires and cables that are easy to trip over. Remove or tape or tack them along the walls as much as possible. Check all appliance cords for fraying and other signs of wear (or, in my case, chew marks from an oral-compulsive cat), and replace the cord, or if necessary, the appliance.

Extension cords are for temporary use only. They are not intended to replace permanent wiring. Consider hiring an electrician to install more electrical outlets, which will help to prevent the overuse of extension cords. When extension cords must be used, avoid running them under rugs, where they may be damaged by furniture or foot traffic.

Also ensure that table lamps are weighted and balanced, making them hard to knock over. In addition, you can tack them into place using a reversible adhesive, such as Blu-Tack.

Periodically test and reset ground-fault circuit interrupter (GFCI) outlets and breakers to ensure they are functioning properly.

Many people use portable space heaters to augment their home's central heating. Before using a space heater, replace older models with modern units, which are safer and more efficient. Always read and follow the manufacturer's instructions, as well as any warnings attached to the appliance. Keep space heaters at least 3 feet (1 meter) away from anything that can burn, including living creatures.

The oven should not be used as a source of heat. Gas stoves in particular can produce deadly levels of carbon monoxide. To prevent carbon monoxide buildup, have all fuel-burning appliances inspected annually, including the furnace, fireplace or woodstove, damper and chimney. Install carbon monoxide alarms on each level of the home.

If the home is truly chilly and heating bills are too high, buy warmer clothes, socks and house shoes, and provide extra throws and small blankets in common seating areas, along with down comforters and blankets in the bedroom. Electric blankets are another potential hazard, both in terms of overheating or burning fragile older skin (especially if someone can't sense high heat) and in terms of the electricity itself (especially if left on overnight). Improve home insulation to forestall the desire to use space heaters, and humidify to make dry heat feel more comfortable.

Butt Out: Prevent Smoking-Related Fires

Quit smoking. Help the people you love quit smoking. Of course, we know it's not that simple, especially for people who are heavily addicted to nicotine. For so many reasons, though, it's important to quit, so ask the doctor about enrollment in a supervised quit-smoking program. There are more tools and support for quitting than ever before, and often it takes a few tries.

When someone you love smokes, or if you smoke, create and enforce rules about the time and place for smoking—preferably outside. *Never* smoke in bed or in an upholstered chair or sofa, or anywhere a smoker might get drowsy and nod off.

Many fires are started by smoking materials not quite going out, so proper disposal of ashes and butts is critical. Smokers should put out their cigarette butts completely. You might use signs instructing smokers to completely extinguish their cigarettes, as in a place of business. In assigned smoking areas, place deep (emptied) ashtrays or small buckets of sand for adequate disposal. Small metal cans used solely for used or discarded cigarettes and matches could also be helpful.

If you suspect that cognitive changes may be affecting a smoker's ability to handle lit cigarettes safely, please talk to his or her doctor. At some point, you may have to remove or hide the cigarettes and matches.

Hot Stuff: Prevent Heat-Related Injury

Help yourself and your loved ones stay out of hot water. To avoid accidental scalds, which are as dangerous as burns from flames, set the hot-water heater to the recommended maximum temperature of 120° F (49° C). And caution older people to always check water temperature before getting into the bathtub or shower. Anti-scald devices on faucets can help to prevent scalds (a burn from hot liquid or gas) due to changes in water pressure.

In the kitchen, long, heat-resistant oven mitts work much better than potholders to help cooks grip hot containers and protect against splatters and steam. Hint: They also make nice hostess gifts.

When it comes to steam radiators or any other exposed hot surfaces, cover them with insulating material or barricade them with pieces of furniture.

Waxing and Waning: Blow Out the Candles

Finally, we live in a time of trendy candles, using them for fragrance and an intimate ambiance. Candles, however, can quickly turn a house into a death trap. If they tend to help people relax, those same relaxed people can nod off or leave them unattended. As a result, they're a leading cause of home fires, according to the AARP (formerly the American Association of Retired Persons).

Flameless, battery-operated candles are a great alternative and come in many shapes, styles and even scents. They're sold in gift shops, department stores, even supermarkets—pretty much anywhere you can buy regular candles. The most common ones look like chunky wax candles and use special LED bulbs to simulate a flickering flame.

Aromatic alternatives to candles include potpourri and fragrance beads.

——— ◆ ———

What happened to Betty the cook, who opened this chapter? Her family built up her staying power in several subtle ways. Her daughter-in-law tactfully suggested that they cook together more often and separately asked her older children to keep an eye on Grandma. She placed a loud, easy-to-read timer next to the stove and made sure that nearby smoke detectors had fresh batteries. As an inducement for Betty to stay in the kitchen while things cooked, she set a basket with some colorful magazines on the table nearby. And she talked to her husband privately about taking Betty to the doctor to discuss the changes in her memory.

LET'S GET STARTED

Top Tips for a Smoke-Free Home

____ Take inventory of flammable and hazardous materials, label them clearly, and store them away from heat and flame.

____ Post 911 and other emergency numbers in the kitchen and next to every phone.

____ Install smoke and carbon monoxide (CO) alarms.

____ Record and observe a test schedule.

____ Post a home fire escape plan and conduct fire safety drills.

____ Check and secure all electrical cords.

____ Replace worn and frayed cords.

____ Use appropriate power strips and GFCI outlets.

____ Weight and/or tack down table lamps.

____ Replace old space heaters with modern ones and follow all manufacturer's instructions and warnings.

____ Place hair ties or nets in a container near the stove.

____ Use a loud kitchen timer.

____ Place a large pot lid near the stove.

____ Do not smoke inside the home.

____ Set hot-water temperature to safe levels (120° F/49° C).

____ Install anti-scald devices.

☑ LET'S GO SHOPPING
Top Tools for a Smoke-Free Home

- ☐ Smoke alarms with "hush" buttons or alarm-pause features for every story and outside sleeping areas
- ☐ Carbon monoxide alarms for every level
- ☐ Power strips with automatic breakers
- ☐ GFCI outlets as needed, usually for wet areas, such as near the kitchen and bathroom sinks
- ☐ Loud kitchen timers
- ☐ Anti-scald devices
- ☐ Flameless candles instead of real ones

Chapter 4

The Easy Home:
Function and Mobility

N*ancy retired from her career as an accountant in San Diego and looked forward to an enjoyable retirement helping with the grandkids, fixing things around the house, and cooking all those dishes she never had time for before. Unfortunately, her hands didn't share her excitement. They tingled or felt numb, which the doctor said was carpal tunnel syndrome from years of keyboard use. Adding insult to injury, she developed arthritis in her hands as well. They felt so stiff and sore. So much for those hobbies.*

Meanwhile, a year after her husband, Jim, died of cancer, Nancy's cousin Susie felt ready to leave their home of 25 years in Brampton, Ontario, and downsize. She wanted to stay near her friends and settled on a new townhouse a short drive away. But she, like her cousin Nancy, is grappling with challenges to her staying power. Shortly after moving in, she fell on the ice and twisted her knee. Now she's in rehab. All those stairs are exhausting, and it's hard to move around the cute little house with the walker, the crutches and the cane. Susie wonders if the future is going to bring more of the same. Is she going to be trapped in her own home?

---- ◆ ----

As these stories illustrate, age often brings some kind of disability. That may not be a pleasant word to hear, but before you slam this book shut, at least wait to find out what it really means.

First, a disability is not, in itself, a disease. A disability is something that limits a person's mobility, hearing, vision, speech or mental function.

Resulting from accidents, trauma, genetics or disease, disabilities are often seen in old age because older people are more prone to having disabling conditions, such as arthritis.

Old age is not automatically disabling. Remember, anyone can land on the disabled list, at any time. Professional and weekend athletes, the accident-prone and the unlucky can cycle in and out of disability at any age. It's more that age-related conditions such as arthritis or macular degeneration can limit prior ability. Old age raises the odds.

Thus, likely because of the population aging, the number of Americans reporting a disability rose in the last decade to roughly 1 in 5, according to the latest figures from the U.S. Centers for Disease Control and Prevention. The leading cause of disability was arthritis (8.6 million people), followed by back or spine problems (7.6 million), and heart trouble (3 million). As the population ages, those numbers are expected to rise.

We can try to prevent disability by staying active, keeping a healthy weight and avoiding smoking. Even so, despite our best efforts, the years may still bring some reduction in ability. Your assignment, should you choose to accept it? Try to take the "dis" out of disability. It is simply a different type or level of ability—no disrespect needed or intended.

Better yet, it doesn't have to be a problem, thanks to an abundance of clever tools and compensatory techniques. Universal Design (remember this from Chapter 1?) teaches us that what is good for people with disabilities is good for everyone.

As someone without a major disability who lived happily in a one-level house using D-shaped cabinet handles, 100 percent rocker switches, a grab bar in the tub, and a big-buttoned kitchen phone (what can I say, I'm lazy), I'll vouch for that.

Joint Action: The Biggest Disabler

Arthritis is the leading cause of disability in old age. Surprised? Arthritis is like the common cold of the musculoskeletal system. It happens a lot, makes people miserable and hurts productivity more than we know. Look at the numbers: According to the Centers for Disease Control and Prevention, osteoarthritis (the most common form of the disease) affects every other person over the age of 65.

In arthritis, decades of use and abuse influence how our joints work. One change that occurs is the wearing out of the cartilage that protects our joints and keeps them smoothly bending and flexing. Cartilage is the soft, rubbery material that, in younger people, keeps bone ends from rubbing against each other during normal movement. Unprotected bones will grate and grind instead. Ouch! No wonder arthritis means pain, inflammation and stiffness.

Carrying excess weight puts extra stress on the joints. In fact, losing just 10 pounds can reduce the pressure on your knees, hips and spine by the equivalent of 40 pounds. And, according to the Arthritis Foundation, osteoarthritis can damage not only the bone ends in the joints, but also muscles, tendons (which connect muscles to bones), ligaments (which connect bones to bones across a joint) and the knees' extra rings of cushion, called menisci.

Whatever the cause, osteoarthritis can restrict range of motion, making it harder to exercise and carry out everyday activities. Osteoarthritis tends to strike the hips, knees, hands, ankles and shoulders—just the joints we need to get things done, from writing checks to cooking meals, climbing stairs and rolling over in bed.

Rheumatoid arthritis, although much less common than osteoarthritis, can also be very disabling. This chronic inflammatory disease of the joints flares up, somewhat unpredictably, when the immune system mistakenly attacks the lining of the joints. Unlike osteoarthritis, the rheumatoid form is usually symmetrical, affecting the same joint on each side. It flares up nearly anywhere except the hips.

Other arthritic conditions, such as gout and fibromyalgia, can limit pain-free movement too. Other age-related conditions can also limit the ability to move freely and securely. In addition, Parkinson's disease and the milder Essential Tremor can affect strength and flexibility, including in the hands.

The bottom line for all of the above is that joint and movement disorders cause a wide range of problems in everyday life. People hobble along on rusty knees, struggle to open jars of food, shake their water glass at the table, and fumble to get out of the car. Chronic pain wears people down, causing fatigue.

Got arthritis? Chant along with me: "Motion is lotion." Cranking up the joints may take extra effort to overcome stiffness and pain, but our joint tissues are designed to be mechanically active and work together. Motion kick-starts the process and also oils the joints by warming and spreading the natural lubricant called synovial fluid (which arthritis also affects). The synovial fluid reduces friction and pain.

Thus, it is essential to adapt a home in a way that makes it more possible to keep moving and doing as much as possible, whether via stairs, ramps, door handles, and/or special tools.

Anyone with arthritis pain should talk to the doctor about treatment, weight reduction if required, and exercise. Although it might seem counterintuitive, a supervised program of weight training can strengthen the muscles that support the joints, thus reducing the load that causes joint pain. Muscles can become smaller, hence weaker, from inactivity or as a natural part of aging (after age 65, that shrinkage is called sarcopenia). Keeping them strong is critical for keeping arthritic joints functioning.

See Chapter 6 to learn more about home-based exercise, including muscle-building strength training.

2-4-6-8: Who Do We Accommodate?

Arthritis and other physical, musculoskeletal and neuromuscular problems are only disabling relative to how much they limit our ability to do what we want to do. As a result, the good news is that people can recruit an army of aids to improve daily life. Making things easier frees energy to use for more important things. That energy is precious.

For instance, when a woman walks into an empty room or down a darkened hall, she doesn't want to have to think, "Now which switch is this one? How should I flex my wrist and curl my fingers?" Multiply that thought and awkward posturing by the number of times she turns the light on or off per day to see how having uniform light switches can boost her personal energy savings.

For a common problem like weak hands and wrists, assistive devices are wonderful. Home health and regular drugstores, kitchen stores, and other outlets (including online) stock the kinds of simple tools that boost quality of life. Take a special trip to browse the offerings: You may be pleasantly surprised at the possibilities. Here are just some of the available tools:

+ Rotating lamp-switch extenders with large three-spoke knobs help people with limited grasp.
+ Vertical light-switch extenders sold for use by children are handy for people in wheelchairs.

- ✦ Doorknob turners lock onto knobs and give you an easier-to-turn lever handle (or you can replace the doorknob altogether).
- ✦ L-shaped handles transform everything from stove-top dials to round faucets.
- ✦ Crank adapters make opening windows easier.
- ✦ Motorized switches open and close heavy window coverings.

Everyday appliances can save personal energy, too, such as an electric can opener, a small food processor, or a lightweight vacuum cleaner.

To review the many opportunities to accommodate arthritic or related problems, let's start with the most challenging areas, the kitchen and bathroom, and move on to other aspects of access and mobility.

IN THE KITCHEN

Given the many hours people spend in their kitchens cooking and cleaning, and the centrality of good food and company to our quality of life, this is the place to start.

Food Preparation and Storage

Most good housewares stores now carry kitchen tools with large cushioned grips and improved design. Store the most commonly used tools at or near their point of use. Everyday items can also go in shallow baskets installed inside deeper drawers.

Replace drawer knobs with D-shaped pull handles, which are much easier to grasp. All it takes is a screwdriver and a drill to make the extra hole. If you can open cabinet doors with knobs easily, a switch might not be needed. Magnetic, push or self-closing latches may reduce the energy needed to open and close cupboard doors and drawers.

Glass doors or open shelves in upper cabinets lessen the work required to see, store and remove needed items.

Pull-out or roll-out storage shelves, wire baskets and waste and recycling bins in cabinets can be purchased off the shelf or custom-made. All reduce the need to bend and lift. They also save energy and free up floor space.

Pictures make it easy to see the possibilities.

Photo courtesy of ShelfGenie®

Photo courtesy of ShelfGenie®

Floor pedals can also be installed on items like roll-out trash or recycling bins, again reducing the need to bend.

A kitchen chair or a stool can help the cook sit and save energy during lengthier tasks. Work surfaces can be adjusted to make things easier, too. If you or your folks can remodel, countertops can be raised or lowered. In fact, Universal Design (see Chapter 1) kitchens have counters or work surfaces at heights comfortable for either standing or sitting, and to accommodate people of varying heights and conditions. Common counter heights are 30, 36 and 42 inches off the floor. If it's not possible to change the height of the counter, a nearby table can come in handy for preparing food.

Base (below the counter) cabinets can be (re)configured with open areas for leg space for people seated in chairs or wheelchairs. Even sink heights can be adjusted. To prevent leg burns, insulate exposed hot water pipes.

The right appliances can help as well. Some newer refrigerators and ovens are easier to open due to more and smaller doors, and side-by-side refrigerators minimize reaching too high or stooping too low. Ideally, the oven and microwave should be installed at a height that doesn't require bending or reaching above shoulder height, with side-hinged doors that allow people to sit, perhaps in a chair, while accessing the interior.

Maintain an open counter space very close to the microwave and oven, to allow users to safely remove and place hot and heavy items.

Dining In

Special high-grip utensils and plates provide security to help with anything from muscle weakness to tremors. Or go the do-it-yourself route and fatten up handles with foam cylinders available in hardware and plumbing supply stores. Plates with rims may be easier to use, along with lighter pots. Dollar stores are good for rubberized mesh place mats, as well as rubberized disks useful for both protecting stored dinner plates and holding them in place during a meal or on a tray. Also, look for large-handled flatware and rocker knives that have large curved blades, the latter good for one-handed cutting.

Washing Up

Install single-lever faucets in the kitchen (and bath). People with compromised fine-motor skills find them so much easier to use. Look for something you can shut off with a forearm or the side of your hand, and make sure the appliance meets ADA standards (ADA stands for the Americans With Disabilities Act, which sets standards for barrier-free living). There's even a faucet that turns on and off when tapped on the spout or handle. Scald controls (mentioned in Chapter 3) can help prevent burns.

People who are worried about dropping dishes when washing them by hand can switch to melamine (a nice plastic) or tempered glass (which doesn't exactly bounce but is light and breaks less easily). Let the user see what feels right. It may also help to wash dishes and clean up in shorter, more frequent shifts.

Look into whether you can raise the dishwasher to 42 inches high, or install dishwasher drawers that can sit just below the counter.

IN THE BATHROOM

Washrooms are strange, aren't they? They're all slick and shiny with oddly shaped fixtures, yet what would we do without them? Use an outhouse? Squat over a hole in the ground? Here's how to adapt the bathroom for safer and more comfortable use.

Save Energy

People with hip and knee problems or overall reduced lower-body strength may benefit from raised "comfort height" toilets, sold in plumbing supply and some big-box stores. (They're also easier for healthy people who are average or above-average in height.) An existing toilet can also be made higher with a riser installed below the toilet or one installed between the bowl and seat or a molded-plastic, raised seat attached to the toilet. Typically, risers elevate toilet seats by 3 to 5 inches. There's even a fancy (and costly) toilet seat equipped with a built-in night light and motorized seat that rises at the touch of a button and heats up, too. No kidding.

It's easier to slide shower curtains than heavy glass doors. Instead of using a tension rod, bolt a regular rod into the wall. (Use anchors or screw it into the studs.) More translucent, less opaque shower curtains will let in more light. To add light for greater safety and convenience in a dark shower area, ask an electrician to install a recessed vapor-proof fixture.

To further conserve energy or address problems with hand weakness or coordination, older people can use bath mitts and soap-on-a-rope, along with bath and hair- and tooth-care products in pump dispensers. Wall-mounted soap dispensers in the bath keep people from stooping to pick up soap. Dental hygiene might go easier with large-handled electric toothbrushes, flossing swords and water pics. A terry-cloth bathrobe can reduce the energy and flexibility needed to towel off.

If storage is hard to reach, perhaps you can install drawers or caddies on the sides of the sink, or lower down the wall. A tilting or magnifying mirror, perhaps on an expanding frame, will allow people to see themselves without bending. To save energy during tasks such as pedicures or the application of skin lotion, consider extending the tub with a flat ledge for sitting. At least, if space permits, add a bathroom-friendly chair or stool with nonslip feet in a dry spot.

Again, as in the kitchen, sinks that either adjust in height or suit the user's height can come in handy. Double sinks work well if one is lower for sitting. Pedestal sinks allow close-in access to the basin. Wall-mount sinks with leg access require insulation of the hot water pipes underneath.

Prevent Falls

Properly installed grab bars (discussed in detail in Chapter 2) can help people get on and off the toilet. An occupational or physical therapist can advise you on proper placement for your space. Some wall-mounted support bars swing out of the way.

Toilet safety rails help prevent falls and, in case of a slip, they give people something to hold onto instead of pulling on towels and shower curtains. And although hard toilet seats are less comfy, opt for them instead of slippery cushioned seats.

Transfer benches with suction feet help people get in and out of the tub safely. These lightweight benches straddle the side of the tub, allowing people to sit on the bench outside the tub and swing their legs in, rather than having to step into the tub. These photos show two different types.

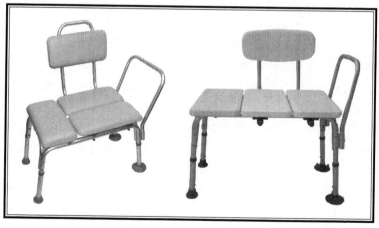

Photo courtesy of Cardinal Health Canada

A shower chair or bench is used when they can step into the tub or shower stall (with a grab bar). Some people install wall-mounted shower seats that fold out of the way, but once mounted, these are not adjustable like freestanding seats. Handheld shower heads make it easier to shampoo and rinse.

Because bathroom surfaces are hard and head injury is always a concern, see if a contractor can smooth out sharp edges and corners of countertops to ease the impact of a potential blow.

Finally, given the high percentage of falls that transpire in the bathroom, consider installing an emergency call button or phone in the bathroom, or set up a dry area to park a mobile phone.

Mobility: Getting Up and Going Down

Has it started? You know . . . those little knee crackles when you bend. The *whoomph* when you collapse into a chair (loud sigh optional). Leaning on the stair rails when you *schlep* up the stairs. Do you notice? Are you embarrassed? Or do you think it's cute?

Unless we maintain muscle strength (which we lose if we do nothing) and our joints cooperate, getting up and going down get harder as we age. Even with exercise and a healthy weight, joints still tend to wear out. Early injuries come back to haunt us. Weekend sports (I'm talking about you, fellow boomers!) take a toll.

Watch your loved ones: Are they *oomphing* and *whoomphing* their way through life? Maybe there are some things you can change around the house to reduce the demands of this type of movement and enable folks to keep their balance.

Furniture with wide, sturdy armrests and high backs helps people support themselves as they go up and down. Remove casters or lock the wheels, and eliminate furniture with legs that curve outward as well. Repair any broken or wobbly furniture.

Higher seats and beds are easier to manage than lower pieces. To determine the correct height for a piece of furniture, measure the distance from the floor to the top of the prospective user's knee cap while standing. That's the optimal height for a piece of seating, from the floor to the top of the seat. Double check the height of a piece of furniture by having its primary user sit on it and test the ease of getting up and down. Take a similar approach with dressers and wardrobes, and get a whole new look in the process.

You can raise furniture in various ways. If it's too soon to redecorate, add firm seat cushions instead. Concerned about appearance? Purchase high-density foam cut to measure and sew a slipcover (or get one made) to match the existing fabric.

For a firmer solution, use blocks under chair and sofa legs. Blocks about 4 inches high with cavities for furniture or bed feet are sold in major home-furnishings chains and online stores (search for bed blocks/bed-riser blocks). Available at larger home and medical supply stores, these are often used to elevate the upper body to reduce the upward flow of acid reflux. You can double the number to elevate all four feet. Blocks with cavities are secure, or you can glue on or screw in the blocks.

Never place furniture on blocks without securing them to the main piece.

Inexpensive padded swivel seats, sold online for less than 30 smackers, can help people to rotate and get up. This can be especially useful in rising from low seating.

Special pneumatic uplift chair seats are also on the market. Look online for "chairs that lift" or "uplift cushions."

Then there's the rocking chair, a staple of the golden-years scenario. Though they may offer tranquil moments on the porch, rocking chairs are unstable and present a tripping hazard. Gliders are unstable when leaned on.

For getting in and out of bed, short bed rails can help sleepy people stay steady. While you're at it, check to see that the path from bed to bathroom is clear. Some people may be better off using a bedside commode.

For serious help with stairs, consider interior stair lifts. Powered by rechargeable batteries or household electrical current, stair lifts are made for either straight or curved stairs and fitted to stair treads, which must be in good enough shape for installation. Lifts vary: Some provide a chair on rails and lift only the person, who transfers in and out. Heavy-duty lifts can carry a wheelchair as well. In any case, check the lift's weight limit. A reliable medical equipment provider can ensure that a lift meets the safety codes established by the American Society of Mechanical Engineers (www.asme.org).

Finally, here's a tip for people having problems getting up and down: In any room, check that occupants can easily reach wall switches and electrical outlets. Outlets can be moved to or newly installed at 27 inches or more off the floor, and at counter height in the kitchen and bath.

Safety note: In wet areas, always install and routinely test GFCI outlets—ground-fault circuit interrupters that prevent shock or electrocution.

Accessibility: The Ins and Outs

People fortunate enough to live in one-level homes with open designs that have wide door openings and exterior doors at ground level (or entry ramps built to code) are exceedingly lucky. These houses are appallingly rare. Most houses are not very accommodating, so the rest of us will make do, remodel, buy stair lifts or move.

First, make sure that doorsills, or thresholds, are smooth and continuous to prevent tripping hazards for feet, cane tips and walkers, and to make it easier for wheelchairs. A carpenter or contractor can obtain wood strips with diet-book names like "overlap reducer" and "flush reducer" to ensure safe and continuous passage from one room to the next. Check metal strips for evenness and hammer down protruding nails.

Doorways need to be at least 32 inches wide; 36 inches is better. In work spaces, wheelchairs require a 5-foot turning radius.

To widen doorways, the simplest fix is offset hinges, which add 2 inches. A bigger fix: pocket doors that slide into the walls, either all to one side or split between the two sides. Look for high-quality ball bearings on the tracks, and add a large D-shaped door pull. Decorative side panels on exterior doors can be removed to allow for the installation of wider doors, or two narrower doors that together create a wide opening.

Should you change doors, tell the installer to make sure the bathroom door, in particular, opens out into the hall so that if someone should fall against the door, helpers can get in. To avoid trapping people, swap out a locking knob for a regular one.

To further adapt a multilevel home for single-level living, consider whether a main-floor den or formal dining room can be turned into a bedroom. A powder room might be expanded to include roll-in showers, particularly if it's adjacent to a convertible hall closet.

Although that entails some remodeling expense, many homeowners weigh that against the cost of moving somewhere else. The other floors won't go to waste: They can be used for visitors, storage, and, perhaps over time, live-in health aides.

Whatever the setting, arrange the furniture to allow maximum ease in getting around. Toss out preconceived notions of how space is supposed to be used. Ensure at least 36 inches of open space in and around furniture for easy passage, especially via walker or wheelchair. Remove any low items, such as step stools, that might block access—and might not be easily seen.

Hallways and other interior pathways should also be at least 36 inches wide. Note that light paint and adequate overhead lighting increase contrast and visibility, making it easier to move around these often darker spaces. Also check the sides of doors and openings to ensure that nothing potentially harmful sticks out at any level.

For residents using a wheelchair or walker, create a special storage area to keep it safely out of the way and remove wheelchair footplates when it's not in use. Special matting can protect the floor from heavy use.

In any dining space, check how easily chairs can be moved. Too heavy, and they'll be hard for frailer diners. Too light, and diners can go skittering off. Installing chair glides on chair legs can reduce friction against the floor. Leg casters might be hazardous and remove that all-important "something to push against" for getting up from furniture. Again, adequate space around the chairs will help everyone take a seat at the table.

Finally, in public areas where privacy, light and sound are not issues, doors can be removed altogether.

— ◆ —

Let's see how the ladies who opened this chapter leveraged their staying power. Nancy investigated both medical and surgical options to relieve her carpal tunnel syndrome. She undertook physical therapy. To reduce her keyboarding time, she added voice-recognition software and a microphone to her computer and started using the microphone option to enter text on her smartphone. She replaced old kitchen tools with new ones that had wider, cushioned grips. And on the advice of her physical therapist, she kept some rubber balls by the TV and did hand exercises every day.

Her cousin Susie, meanwhile, traded in her old Victorian sofa for a new, easy-to-handle sofa bed so she could sleep downstairs for the duration. She also looked into the possibility of renting a chair lift for the stairs. In that case, the sofa bed can accommodate friends, relatives (company during the slow healing process) or even a caregiver. These steps relieved some of her anxiety and bought her time to consider her options.

A Picture Speaks a Thousand Accessible Words

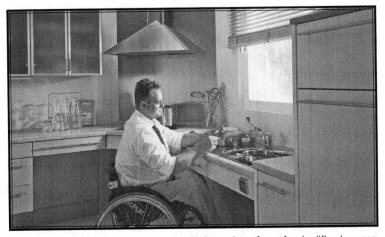

Photo courtesy of www.freedomliftsystems.com

Why do I like this picture so much? Is it because . . .

+ It shows an "accessible" kitchen that allows a person in a wheelchair to use a shallow sink?
+ The pipes are in the back and insulated to prevent him from burning his legs?

✦ The sink has a single-lever tap that can be controlled by a fist or the side of the hand, eliminating the need for precise finger movements that can be difficult or painful for people with arthritis?

✦ The lever is long, reducing the reaching and bending required by short-handled taps?

✦ The sink has a built-in drain board angled for excess water to drain into the basin, requiring less energy to wipe the counter?

Why do I like this picture so much? The answer is "none of the above." I like it because it shows a man who came home from work and started cooking dinner right away.

LET'S GET STARTED

Top Tips for an Easy Home

____ Rearrange furniture for easy clearance.

____ Widen doorways as needed.

____ Make sure all door thresholds are level.

____ Store heavy/breakable items lower.

____ Assess cookware and dishes for weight and fragility; replace as needed.

____ Use pull-out drawers and racks.

____ Replace knobs with large, color-contrasting D-shaped handles.

____ Replace split hot/cold-turning faucet controls with one-lever, ADA-compliant faucets.

____ Install rocker light switches.

____ Use doorknob turners and light-switch extenders.

____ Insulate exposed hot water pipes (this is more for safety).

☑ **LET'S GO SHOPPING**

Top Tools for an Easy Home

Controlling

☐ Anything with big buttons

☐ Lamp switch, wall switch and dial extenders

☐ New cabinet/cupboard hardware

☐ Lever faucet/tap handles

Reaching

☐ Lightweight aluminum reachers (jaws + squeeze handles)

☐ Long-handled metal shoe horns

☐ Ladles and backscratchers to pull light items forward

☐ Handheld showerhead

☐ Extendable, tilting and magnifying mirrors

Holding and Handling

☐ Rubberized, extra-long oven mitts

☐ Kitchen tools with oversized cushioned grips

☐ Silicon/nonslip placemats

☐ Plastic or tempered-glass dishware

☐ Large-handled flatware, rocker knives

Moving

- ☐ Bed rails
- ☐ Nonslip mats
- ☐ Grab bars
- ☐ Transfer bench

Using

- ☐ Insulation for hot water pipes
- ☐ Toilet seat risers and extenders
- ☐ Bath/shower chair

Chapter 5

The Sensitive Home:
Eyes, Ears and More

Mark drove a delivery truck for an overnight-delivery company, so it was especially cruel when he developed macular degeneration and had to give up his license. Public transportation in his Atlanta suburb is spotty, and he misses his independence. Meanwhile, his husband, David, isn't what you'd call a great cook. Mark doesn't want to spend his days stumbling around his own house, listening to books on tape, eating frozen food, watching his staying power dwindle away and getting more and more dependent.

— ◆ —

See me . . . hear me . . . touch me . . . things around the house cry out to be sensed. If only it were so easy. Aging alters the five senses in ways that require adjustment to be living in the material world. However, people whose sensory limitations started early have blazed a trail for people whose first experience of limited *anything* comes only with advancing years. They and the people who work with them have invented or developed a wide array of resources that can help anyone live more comfortably with sensory issues.

To get a feel for how early the senses change, hearing starts to go in the mid-40s, vision and touch in the mid-50s, taste in the mid-60s, and smell in the mid-70s. So, barring a medical condition, you can sequence the adaptations—hearing first, vision second and so on.

To learn how to reshape the home environment as things change, let's review the five senses in order of how they change with age.

Can You Hear Me Now?

Despite the stereotypes about old folks and deafness, it doesn't happen to everyone. The National Institutes of Health report that about half of people over age 75 have some degree of age-related hearing loss, called presbycusis, which makes it hard to hear, especially in noisy surroundings. High-frequency sounds disappear first, due to the loss of certain types of hair cells deep inside our ears.

Normally, the ear's specialized hair cells quiver like Elvis Presley's hips in response to sound waves rocking the fluid of the inner ear. When those hair cells get altered by advancing age, or they're damaged or killed off by high-decibel noise exposure, they cannot send as much sound to the brain. With less transmission comes less translation, because what little sound gets through might be distorted.

That's why, with age-related hearing loss, other people's voices can sound mumbled or slurred, making conversation difficult. Some people even get a little paranoid because they think that others are whispering behind their backs. The loss is usually progressive and irreversible. Hearing loss may also be accompanied by tinnitus, a high-pitched ringing in the ears in the absence of external sound. (Tinnitus is thought to affect more than 1 in 3 older adults.)

At home, hearing is important not only for daily living (you want to talk to people, pick up the phone and answer the door) but also for safety and socializing.

To help people who have hearing loss, reduce the overall sound level in the home and make it easier to talk, hear the doorbell, and enjoy music and TV. Turn off any unnecessary competing sounds whenever possible, especially during conversations. Lined or insulating drapes, carpeting (not too plush; see Chapter 2), and other sound-absorbing materials can help make a kind of hush all over your world. Quieter appliances also help.

Overhead lighting makes it easier for people with hearing loss to see talkers' faces and augment what they hear by "reading" speech from lips, facial expression and gestures. Chairs placed directly across from each other foster better conversation.

To counter general hearing loss, amplification via hearing aids can be a big help. This more selective approach to amplification can keep the home from shaking to the rafters, especially if one partner has better hearing than the other. That avoids your amping up the local soundtrack. Be a good neighor.

Specialized phones, doorbells and timers, as well as assistive listening devices for the TV and other electronics, can improve hearing or alert people with hearing loss in tones that are more audible to older ears. Vibrating alarm clocks stashed under bed pillows awaken sleepers on time. Alerting systems are great when used in phones, doorbells and door chimes, smoke and carbon monoxide detectors and even baby monitors. Test all alarms in the home to ensure that users can hear them, especially from their bedrooms.

The use of captioning when watching live or recorded TV programs or films can lessen the need to turn up the volume. Warn wearers about personal music players: They're wonderful, but it's too easy to crank up the volume to levels that damage hearing even more because those tiny earplugs don't block ambient sound. (Noise-canceling headphones may help if used appropriately.) More important, personal players reduce the ability to attend to the surroundings. Please discourage their use in the kitchen, on the stairs or outdoors.

Finally, even if they can't fully restore normal hearing, hearing aids can help a lot. Encourage people over the age of 65 to visit an audiologist, obtain a baseline screening exam, and follow changes over time. If they wear hearing aids, check on battery life and provide fresh batteries as needed. To ensure comfort and optimal benefit, be sure that hearing aids are properly selected and fitted by an audiologist.

The Vision Thing

Normal vision changes with age. Most obviously, people typically get more far-sighted and start reaching for the reading glasses.

The eyes also take in less light, due to smaller pupil size and a yellowing, thickening lens. According to Lighthouse International, a 60-year-old receives only about 40% of the same amount of available light as a young adult. People in the older group need two to three times as much light as before to see well.

Older people also have a lower tolerance for glare, are less able to adapt to big changes in brightness (such as going out into the bright sun or into a dark house), can't see things as clearly, and find it harder to focus on objects at different distances or even correctly judge distances. Color vision and contrast sensitivity are also affected.

To top it off (so to speak), as people shrink in height from spinal compression or wheelchair use, their point of view drops down.

As a result, older people can develop more problems with everything from finding their way to keeping a secure footing. They need enough light to enter a home and carry out tasks safely, more visual cues to feel secure about where they put their feet, and better access to lighting and lighting controls.

To begin with, everyone needs regular eye exams and, if necessary, to wear accurate, up-to-date corrective lenses. The pace of vision degeneration slows in middle age, but change can still happen and sometimes signal the onset of something more serious. Older people should have regular checkups for glaucoma (pressure inside the eye) and other age-related vision problems.

Prevention is the key. Are sunglasses being worn? With older eyes sensitive to glare, maybe everyone can get a gift of wrap-around sunshields (which are starting to come in different sizes and styles to prevent that bug-eyed look), polarized to reduce glare and treated to block harmful ultraviolet rays.

A nutrient-rich diet is thought to support eye health. In fact, a large-scale study by the National Eye Institute found that high levels of antioxidants (Vitamins C and E, beta-carotene) and zinc with a little copper for balance significantly reduce the risk (in people known to be at risk) of advanced age-related macular degeneration and its associated vision loss. An additional five-year study is under way.

Blood pressure changes and diabetes can also affect sight, so look out for whether changes such as blurred vision might be a sign of something else.

A good number of older adults experience vision changes that are more significant or even serious, causing them to be visually challenged. The terms used to describe reduced vision go like this:

Blind refers to people who have no functional vision, require Braille to read and travel and use a white cane or service dog.

Legally blind people have acuity in their better eye of 20/200 or worse, and/or their peripheral vision is less than 20 degrees. Acuity is used to determine eligibility for driver's licenses, disability benefits and services for the visually challenged.

Low vision refers to those who don't have clear vision, even with corrective lenses. Even with functional vision, they find it hard to read, perform daily tasks under normal lighting and navigate with ease.

What to do about vision changes in general? Start by increasing the level of light. With a greater light requirement, it's time to lighten up. It's safer and it's also easier on the eyes, which have to work harder to do the same tasks.

Everything is, or must be, illuminated. Brighter bulbs alone won't do it: They may overload the fixtures, add too much heat, use too much energy, and give off an irritating glare. Compact fluorescents offer greater candlepower without these drawbacks. My mother, still a heavy reader in her late 80s, tested these bulbs to her satisfaction.

To make a bigger change, consider adding more overhead lighting to gain even illumination and cover more areas of the room and floor—a safety plus. Just one or two fixtures for indirect lighting might do the trick. If renovations are under way, recessed or pot lights can offer smooth, even lighting that's adjustable by dimmer. Chandeliers are pretty but throw off a lot of reflections and glare. It may be time to hand them down or sell them.

Although you want to add more light, beware of doing it through table and floor lamps that will only create more pockets of light and dark. People sneak in extension cords, which create more tripping hazards.

One day soon, most fluorescents will be dimmable, allowing us to make that light source more pleasing and comfortable. In the meantime, other technologies, such as light-emitting diodes (LEDs), are fast emerging as low-energy alternatives. Talk to an electrician and visit your local lighting store or an online lighting supplier to learn more. Your goal: Hide the direct source of light, soften shadows, and minimize glare and glossy reflections.

Task lighting will remain important. Move the light source closer to the task at hand, whether that's chopping in the kitchen, sewing in the bedroom, or shaving in the bathroom. LED strip or rope lighting can also delineate transitions from one level or area to another, as when it's used on the stairs.

Good lighting in the bathroom and kitchen is important. Ground fault circuit interrupters (GFCIs) are a safety must in the kitchen and bathroom. They prevent shock by instantly shutting down the circuit when electricity comes in contact with water. In the kitchen, overhead lighting is helpful, along with targeted task lighting, for example under the cabinet or cupboard to illuminate common work surfaces. Call the electrician to install a recessed vapor-proof light fixture in the shower.

Easy-to-use or pre-set electronic lighting controls can also be very convenient and reduce the need to turn lights on and off when people enter or leave the home or individual rooms. Even simple motion sensors can make transitions seamless, helpful for entering bathrooms, passing through hallways, and going up and down the stairs. Automatic night lights work wonders, too.

Installing controls at a lower height may make them more accessible. Rocker switches, as explained earlier, are easy on the hands. To heighten contrast and make lighting controls easier to find, install switch plates that contrast with the wall color. And though they've been scorned, clap-on and touch-control lamps are super-easy to use.

Some light switches have a soft, built-in night-light. Consider using these in hallways and bathrooms, and anywhere else frequented during the night. In the bathroom itself, use magnifying mirrors, low-glare lighting and a night light.

Bulbs matter. Full-spectrum bulbs and fluorescents may help reduce glare and eyestrain. Dusting bulbs (when cool!) will maximize the light they emit. Lamps should be simple to clean and placed where they can be easily reached. For any new fixture, consider the ease with which bulbs can be obtained and replaced.

Finally, in case the lights go out, put one working flashlight by the bed and another on the kitchen table. Flashlights are safer than candles. Standing battery-operated lanterns are particularly useful and some can cast a wider beam. Check the batteries monthly.

Optical Illusions

Beyond lighting, other simple changes can help people compensate for diminished vision. Adding contrast between adjacent items can also help people with reduced vision. It's relatively easy and creative to build greater contrast between chairs and floor, eating utensils and the table, curtains/blinds and the window, and so on.

Door trim in a shade that contrasts more strongly with wall color can help people walk safely through openings; wood trim (natural or stained) can also lend contrast. Slipcovers can instantly alter the color of upholstered pieces. Inexpensive pieces can be painted.

In the kitchen, place mats and napkins can set up high contrast with existing dishes. Even the food itself can contrast with the plate or bowl. Avoid clear drinking glasses, and place decals on glass patio doors. Contrasting edges on counters and floors are helpful as well. As was noted in Chapter 2, friction tape not only aids traction but also provides a helpful contrast as to where the stairs begin and end.

To combat changes in visual acuity, post all safety information in large print. Use a combination of Upper- and Lower-Case Letters, which are much easier to read than ALL UPPER CASE. If you are creating instructions using a computer, use **Bold** for better contrast for essential information. If you're writing by hand, use a fatter marker. Especially pay attention to the household "refrigerator numbers," the list of essential day-to-day phone numbers that most people keep somewhere around the house.

Magnifiers, which range in size from wallet-sized to Sherlock Holmes to full page, are very useful. So are talking watches and clocks, large print books (including cookbooks), and so much more.

Use telephones and remote controls with big-button keypads; some are augmented with Braille. Assess computer keyboards and make use of the accessibility settings that come with the operating system software, such as changing the screen settings and using speech recognition.

Newly sophisticated devices employ video and scanning technologies to allow people to view highly magnified text, photos and maps. Commercial equipment is expensive, but handheld video magnifiers and scanner-readers, some of which will read aloud text transferred from a computer, are coming down in price (see the Appendix).

Finally, depending on the degree of vision loss, special tools can make life easier. Home-health stores and online suppliers offer an array of gadgets and gizmos well worth trying, such as big-button telephones and timers. Check them periodically to see what's new.

Limiting Conditions

Beyond general adaptations, specific medical disorders call for targeted solutions.

Age-related *macular degeneration* robs people of the central vision needed to see objects clearly and undertake daily tasks such as reading and driving. This leading cause of legal blindness in Americans 60 and older comes in wet and dry forms and causes no pain. Macular degeneration, which affects the part of the eye that allows us to see fine detail, can advance either slowly or quickly. Bright lights and increased light-dark contrast, such as dark furniture and white walls, can help; so can magnifying equipment. (In the bathroom, consider a bright or contrasting toilet seat.), And, just the other day, I heard of a woman with macular degeneration who relied on her peripheral vision. She cleverly lined the sides of her stairs with white tape so she would know where they were.

Glaucoma is actually a group of eye diseases that result from higher pressure in the eyeball due to fluid buildup. As pressure builds, it damages the retina and the optic nerve to the brain. The National Eye Institute says that people over age 60, especially Mexican Americans, are at risk for glaucoma. The age of heightened risk for African-Americans starts even younger, at 40. Family history also counts, as does diabetes, high blood pressure and anemia. Anyone with one or more of these risk factors should talk to an eye-care professional about regular exams.

Glaucoma is sneaky, affecting side, or peripheral vision, before it progresses to central vision. When you help people with glaucoma, bear in mind that they have tunnel vision and will find it harder to judge things to the side—door frames being the most obvious. Clear the layout of furniture and, perhaps, paint or stain the door frames for a greater contrast with the walls.

Cataracts cloud the lens of the eye, through which light passes to land on the retina. They're most commonly associated with age, although there are other contributing factors, such as diabetes, smoking, and prolonged exposure to sunlight. By age 80, more than half of all Americans either have a cataract or have had cataract surgery, according to the National Eye Institute. Cataracts cause dull and blurry vision, making it harder to see. As cataracts harden, the lens becomes yellowish-brownish, making it harder for people to distinguish blues and purples.

If you know someone with cataracts, look for any blue-purple-black distinctions they may need to make around the house. Try to change the color scheme. Glare is an even bigger problem with cataracts, so cut it down or out however possible.

A Touchy Situation

Age also affects the critical sense of touch, which tells us whether something's too hot or too cold, too heavy or too sharp. Touch helps us dress for the weather and keep out of danger. Yet with aging, thinner, drier skin becomes more sensitive and less elastic. As skin ages, even normally, poor circulation can reduce the sensitivity of the hands and feet. Thinner fat pads in the hands and feet leave them less protected. Nerve damage from various medical conditions can cause numbness and tingling.

Aging also reduces the number of nerve endings, making it hard to feel whether the water's too hot or if there's a cut, blister or other injury that can get infected. It even gets harder to tell things apart, such as coins and buttons, and to handle small objects. Any fine motor skill can be compromised, such as sewing or writing.

Meanwhile, the body's proprioceptive sense of itself relative to its surroundings (a kinesthetic, or movement-related, sense) can also diminish, leaving people off balance. Visual cues and contrast can, as explained in the section on vision, aid orientation in space.

To compensate for the dulling of touch, insulate people from extremes of hot and cold. For example, set the hot water heater at a maximum of 120° F (49° C). Make sure the kitchen has rubber-backed long oven mitts as well as proper ice tongs. Set up a glove-and-mitten depot by the door to remind people to insulate their hands in cold weather. And ensure that people wear appropriate socks.

Old-fashioned rubber fingertips (latex-free in case of allergy) can help with everything from turning pages to sorting coins. Get the best-fitting rubber gloves for washing dishes.

For people who develop dry skin, especially in the winter, humidify the air through individual or whole-house humidifiers. Individual units can be hard to fill, but keeping a spare pitcher, watering can or mixing bowl with a spout on a stable, waterproof surface near the "filling station" can make the job easier. Dry skin can cause itchiness, which leads to scratching, sores and the potential for infection. A pump bottle of hand lotion by every sink will remind washer-uppers to moisturize. A tub of cream at bedside will help with feet and also provide a cue for self-inspection.

Speaking of which, older people should check their skin more frequently for abrasions, discoloration or signs of infection with the aid of a full-length wall mirror (when not inspecting, those who for some reason don't want to see themselves naked all the time can hang a drape or covering with a side tie-back or hook).

Finally, older people have a harder time regulating body temperature, a process essential to optimal function, even survival. Older people run a greater risk of both hypothermia (under-heating) and hyperthermia (over-heating) when exposed to very cold or hot conditions. In the winter, it feels chillier. In the summer, there are more cases of debilitating heat exhaustion and potentially fatal heat stroke. This problem may necessitate using extra blankets and setting the heating thermostat a little higher, even at night. In the increasingly hot summers, ensure adequate air conditioning or fans. Even a bedroom-only air conditioner can promote good health during the hottest part of the day.

Such Good Taste

As we get older, the threshold for "yummy!" gets higher. You may notice that older people don't eat with the old gusto and want more seasoning on their food. That's because the sense of smell is fading and taste buds are going bye-bye. With sweet and salty tastes the first to change, normal seasoning may seem bland.

In response, steer diners away from the over-salting that contributes to high blood pressure. Adding salt at the end instead of the beginning or middle of cooking makes the food taste saltier with a reduced amount. Using fresh garlic in cooking or low-sodium salad dressings also further reduces the need for salt.

Cooks can also use fragrant herbs, salt substitutes such as Mrs. Dash, and stronger spices (if not irritating to the digestive tract) to boost food's sensory allure. A small counter-top or table-top spice rack or carousel can encourage diners to explore new ways to enliven meals. Contrasts in the texture and temperature of food can also make it more appealing. For example, try chewy granola contrasted with smooth yogurt, or a dollop of cool sour cream on warm pureed soup.

Try to prevent "tea-and-toast" syndrome. Diners without the energy to cook a meal can try cereal with milk and fruit (fresh berries, banana slices, dried fruit), a healthier and still simple option. And it's not just young singles that can make great use of grocery store salad bars, with their assorted vegetables, fruit, and protein sources, such as beans, cooked chicken and cheese.

Due to the growing interest in fresh and healthy prepared food, private companies are available in many locations to prepare heart-healthy meals, package them for the freezer and deliver them to the home. To locate them, ask a local dietitian, contact senior services, and look in local "seniors" newspapers and directories. And of course, local Meals on Wheels volunteers continue to deliver daily hot and weekly frozen low-cost meals to eligible people throughout North America. Check online or in your local phone directory.

Consider other ways to pursue and promote good nutrition. Apart from introducing fragrant herbs, spices and sauces, survey the kitchen. A team effort can spruce up the dining area to make it more pleasant. Large-print cookbooks that address special dietary needs or employ a limited number of ingredients might be appreciated.

And simple devices for preserving cooked dishes in the freezer in small one- or two-portion bags can keep meals from getting boring.

Use permanent markers or grease pencils to mark expiration dates on food packages in much larger type than preprinted labels. Maybe a magnifying glass in the kitchen will help. If the storage material or container doesn't hold marks, try a piece of masking tape, enclose the plastic inside a paper bag, or insert a paper label in a rubber band wrapped around the food.

Grocers in larger cities take online orders, enabling people to have fresh food in case of bad weather or if they are ill or disabled. Long-distance caregivers can also use these services for their loved ones. Older people in urban areas might also have duplicate delivery menus. Caregivers: Take the extra menus home and use them to call in deliveries of tasty hot meals, perhaps on special occasions or for a weekly treat. Order extra to provide easy-to-reheat leftovers.

Finally, a medical note to chew on: Good oral hygiene and regular dental checkups are essential to ensure that diners can effectively tear and chew their food.

Changes to the bite over time can diminish the ability to tear, grind and mash food. Large chunks may fall back into the throat, causing problems with swallowing or even choking. The situation may be exacerbated by changes in the muscle tone and diameter of the food tube. Thus, grinding food, whether with properly aligned teeth or mechanical tools such as mortar and pestle, gets more important.

If you suspect any medical or dental changes are getting in the way of a healthy diet, talk to your doctor or dentist or consult an orthodontist.

Sniffing Around

The sense of smell—the oldest sense in our biological history—is imperative to our survival. The smell of smoke or rotten food is as important to us as is the smell of fresh-baked cookies. Transmitting odor molecules to an area of the brain behind the nose, the sense of smell fades a bit with age. A sharp decline is suspected to be associated with Alzheimer's disease, which starts in the region next to the brain's olfactory area.

Sense of smell can help us check the cleanliness level of an older person's home, kitchens, inside the refrigerator, and so on. That person might not notice unpleasant odors, such as from pets, a sensitive subject that has to be tactfully addressed.

Because older people can be less sensitive to the smell of gas or smoke, it's extra-essential to install and maintain smoke and carbon monoxide detectors (see Chapter 3). Kitchen timers are more crucial than ever, along with a comfortable place to sit in the kitchen while things are cooking so the cook isn't tempted to go elsewhere.

———— ✦ ————

Meanwhile, what happened to Mark with his macular degeneration? He embarked on a series of heart-to-heart talks with David about what his condition would mean to their home life. They agreed to install the kinds of lighting and environmental cues that would help Mark stay more indepen-dent, to check out devices that layer auditory cues on top of visuals, and to redecorate to make it easier for him to use (and not knock into) furniture, countertops and tables.

In one fun trip to the housewares store, they stocked up on colorful equipment to help him see more easily in the kitchen and got a magnifier for cookbooks. David agreed to learn to prepare at least a few of Mark's favorite dishes from scratch. Mark, more of a techie, started adjusting his computer screen for greater legibility and learned in advance about big-print books and a much wider selection of audiobooks and podcasts than he had known existed. With changes under way, he pro-moted his staying power and started to accept and feel better about his future.

LET'S GET STARTED

Top Tips for a Sensitive Home

Hearing

____ Use insulated drapes for sound absorption.

____ Arrange the furniture for face-to-face conversation.

____ Use assistive technologies (special phones, doorbells, timers, etc.).

Vision: Increase Light Levels

____ Use fluorescent bulbs, not hotter incandescent bulbs (lower heat and energy costs; incandescent or halogen fixtures might overheat and cause a fire).

____ Use overhead lighting (more even and diffused) and fewer small lamps.

____ Remove hazards that might be missed by people with low vision.

____ Make sure floors are clear and empty.

____ Minimize cords and tack them against the wall.

Vision: Reduce Glare

____ Promote the wearing of sunglasses outside in sun and snow.

_____ Use sheer curtains and shades to cut window glare.

_____ Use indirect lighting, lamp shades and translucent lenses (cover naked bulbs).

_____ With flooring, use a matte/satin finish, not high gloss.

_____ Use soft lighting to balance out the television set (reduce light/dark contrasts).

_____ Place a special (removable) mesh screen over computer monitors.

_____ Place screens (TVs and computers) away from windows.

Vision: Increase Contrast Between . . .

_____ Tables, chairs, sofas and floors

_____ Walls and floors

_____ Doorways and walls

_____ Stair rails/grab bars and walls

_____ Shower curtains and tub/stall tiles

_____ Bath mats and bathtub/floor

_____ Dishes/flatware and place mats/tabletop

_____ Knives and cutting board

_____ Cutting board and countertop

_____ Towels and bathroom/washroom walls

____ Bed linens/covers and the floor

____ Light switches/electrical cover plates and the wall

____ *What else can you think of?*

Touch, Taste and Smell

____ See *Let's Go Shopping*

LET'S GO SHOPPING

Top Tools for a Sensitive Home

Hearing

- [ ] Assistive devices: specialized phones, doorbells, timers; vibrating alarm clocks and so on
- [ ] Sound-muffling insulated drapes

Touch, Taste and Smell

- [ ] Oven mitts
- [ ] Long-handled ice tongs
- [ ] Low-sodium seasonings and sauces
- [ ] Hand lotion in pump bottles

Vision

- [ ] Magnifiers
- [ ] Flashlights
- [ ] Fluorescent, LED, full-spectrum–low-glare, low-wattage bulbs
- [ ] Cord conduit or cord tacks; twist ties
- [ ] Rocker switches
- [ ] Touch-control and clapper lamps
- [ ] Automatic night lights
- [ ] Translucent (low-glare) lighting fixtures
- [ ] Battery-operated lights
- [ ] Two or more flashlights with fresh batteries

- ☐ Wraparound sunshields (UV filters/polarized)
- ☐ Sheer curtains to reduce sun glare
- ☐ Slipcovers
- ☐ Anti-glare mesh screen for computer monitor
- ☐ Any household items—soft and hard goods—that increase contrast
- ☐ Assistive technologies—helpful devices

Chapter 6
The Holistic Home: Mind and Body

Marilyn and Joe felt fortunate they were healthy enough to stay in their four-bedroom Massachusetts home long after their three kids moved out. They finally had space for visitors and hobbies, and the mortgage was paid off. Talk about staying power! Still, a month after being laid up after foot surgery, a stressful time when her blood pressure shot up, Marilyn found she was distracted and forgetful. More and more often, this former math teacher forgot why she went into a room or where her glasses were. And she had to make a real effort to remember to take her pills. Joe got a little worried: Was this Alzheimer's?

People fear falling and losing their independence, but they also dread the prospect of losing their mental faculties. That fear is not unfounded: Experts estimate that roughly half of all people over age 85 are dealing with some degree of cognitive impairment, which means that more and more of us across the generations are affected by Alzheimer's and other types of dementia. Today's middle-aged people are already dealing with progressive memory loss in many of their parents. As a result, their anxiety antennae are alert to any sign of *now what was I about to say*. . . .

It's beyond the scope of this book to discuss how to cope with diagnoses of Alzheimer's disease, or with dementia that involves the vascular system (including mini-strokes or transient ischemic attacks), the brain's frontotemporal lobes or Lewy bodies. Please consult the Appendix to learn about a variety of comprehensive resources that address these concerns.

This book is, instead, for people like Joe and Marilyn. She had no signs of organic disease, so what happened? As it turned out, the combination of stress and inactivity temporarily derailed Marilyn's short-term memory. The pain medicine after surgery made her foggy. She couldn't sleep well, which is bad for the brain. Then, the combination of inactivity and higher blood pressure reduced her circulation, fed her brain less oxygen, and left her bored and a little depressed. Once she was able to move around again, socialize and pursue more stimulating activities, both her mood and her mental function improved.

Marilyn's story is a great reminder that mind and body work together to create a good quality of life. A holistic approach to home life supports both. Thus, this chapter will look at ways to build strong minds and bodies using simple home enhancements.

First, it will look at a few simple ways to compensate for normal mental aging, with sections on special concerns such as fraud prevention and medication management. Second, it will explore options for easy home-based exercise, whose benefits are increasingly shown to strengthen not only the biceps and quadriceps, but mental muscles, too.

Never You Mind: Cognitive Aging

Normal aging can affect the brain just the same as it affects every other part of the body. The maturing mind, consequently, behaves a little differently than it did before. As of this writing, brain scientists don't yet have a perfect picture of what goes on, but enough is known to say the following:

+ Processing speed slows a bit. It takes a little longer to figure things out.
+ Episodic short-term memory—the "what just happened?" of our lives—gets a little worse.
+ Prospective memory—the "remember to buy milk on the way home"—does the same.
+ Executive functioning—getting our mental act together—takes more effort. That's everything from making decisions to setting priorities, from taking initiative to solving problems.
+ Distraction has more power to pull us off track, and it's harder to get back on.

On the plus side, vocabulary and any other well-rehearsed knowledge stick with us, and we know how to use what we have. Words like "good judgment" and "wisdom" start to apply.

Barring disease, it's not that memory goes bad. It's just that it doesn't "pop" like it did in our youth, when constant learning and testing taxed the muscles of memory. With a little more effort, older people can learn. Most important, they can and do slowly adapt to the many gradual changes in ability. For example, people start to group tasks and structure routines in a manner that respects changing energy levels and mental focus.

But there's no grab bar for that. Instead, a variety of simple (and, you may notice, fairly obvious) adaptations and the use of new tools can help with the *"what was I doing again?"* aspect of aging at home. When it comes to common-sense organizing, people tend to be their own best experts. So keep it simple enough to succeed and try it for a few weeks. If it doesn't work, try something else.

You Must Remember This: Memory Aids

It's ridiculously easy to misplace small items around the house. Wearing clothing with plenty of pockets can help. Lightweight house jackets and special vests offer places for keys, a pen and a notebook.

Remember "a place for everything and everything in its place?" A magnificent motto! Storage plays a critical role in the quest for organization, so think about what's getting lost or hard to reach. If organization is not your strong suit, consult an organizing handbook or talk to a professional organizer to develop systems with accessible shelving, hooks, cabinets and cubbies. Cubbies are nice because everything is open to view. As needed, label closed doors and drawers, or add visual cues such as photos of contents.

To further avoid misplacing commonly used items, many people develop the discipline of leaving them in the same place every time *with no exceptions*. For example, reading glasses next to the reading chair; outside glasses on the hall table. At that location, leave eyeglass cases (labeled by wearer if appropriate), or a special felt-lined cup (make one from an old mug) or eyeglass holder as a cue.

Experts also recommend the use of a Memory Book, a kind of home index that lists the locations of commonly used items. For example, "Extra house keys: Drawer next to the kitchen sink." This kind of tool doesn't build dependency or weaken your memory. Instead, it adds a layer of security for memory-zapping times of stress.

Context, a proven aid to memory, fades over time. Older people should develop the habit of taking a few extra seconds to take in the scene surrounding a particular object. (Note to self: Especially useful in big parking lots.)

For people who like gadgets, devices with a base station or more portable units, such as the KeyRinger, activate beepers that are attached to easy-to-misplace personal items such as keys, eyeglasses, cell phones, purses and wallets. To find a cell phone or mobile handset, call it from another phone.

A list is a prime example of a low-tech memory aid that has stood the test of time. Much in the way that braces give external support to the body, lists do the same for your memory. And, like a cane, they help you keep your balance.

Thus, it helps to prepare some standard lists and calendars. For example, a stock grocery shopping list can be created on the computer, organized by category or even by aisle, printed or copied in bulk and hung on the refrigerator with a pencil. Circle items when they run out.

For general shopping, photocopy or print multiples of a template list organized by frequent shopping destinations, such as particular malls or warehouse stores, and/or commonly needed items, such as clothing, toiletries and household items. For example, it's simple to jot items in the "Home and Hardware" or "Drugs and Toiletries" sections. Train everyone to know: "If it's not on the list, it doesn't exist."

Carrying a small notebook with names, important numbers, frequently visited addresses and routes, and annual gift-buying dates (perhaps with sizes and preferences)—whatever is important to the bearer—can be very helpful. It also makes a good place for jotting down information and referrals. Because "source" memory also fades with age, people may want to record the source of the referral, to trace things back or say thank you.

Timers, whether stand-alone or in watches, are helpful, easy to set, and useful for everything from cooking to medicine, meditation breaks, or show-time reminders.

For phoning, it may be helpful and fun to tape pictures of friends and family members onto or next to automatic dial buttons. Voice-activated dialers are also useful. In case of emergency, include 911 on all phone lists. Don't assume callers will remember the number when panicked. For the same reason, post the home's street address in big, clear letters by the phone, along with the name of the nearest intersection and, if applicable, intercom number.

For driving, place index cards or a separate notebook with commonly driven routes and simple local maps or printouts from online mapping sites into the driver's-side pocket or glove compartment. Older people who move somewhere new are especially vulnerable to disorientation and will find it harder to learn new streets. A GPS device isn't necessarily the answer because it can be distracting and doesn't promote active learning of the new area.

Income Property: Work and Hobbies

Modern society is about to retire retirement. As more people live longer, leading more active lives and earning income to match, the concept of traditional retirement is fading fast. At the same time, shrinking pension funds and a volatile economy are further prolonging participation in the labor force.

This demographic shift coincides with the post-industrial breakdown of employment patterns. As jobs disappear (never to return), people are turning to flexible, independent work, often based out of the home.

Thus, it's entirely possible that you or your loved ones will spend decades both aging and working at home.

Many people already plan to work as long as they can, at least part time, to supplement income or to contribute to society or a combination of both motives.

So, although this book isn't about workplace health and safety, the same occupation-specific considerations should apply.

Professionals need to be aware of precautions that apply to their specialty, obtain and use protective equipment, and otherwise play by the rules—whether that means wearing safety goggles when using power equipment for carpentry projects or sitting at the computer in an ergonomic chair.

Speaking of which, working from home often involves the computer. Remember the basics for health and safety: an adjustable chair with lumbar support, a lower keyboard tray, wrist rests for the keyboard, and a mouse or trackball. Position the monitor away from windows and reduce glare by using indirect or task lighting. Some people wear eyeglasses made for computer use, with single-vision prescription lenses adjusted for reading a screen positioned about arm's length from the eyes.

Specialized books (such as the many offerings from home-office pioneers Paul Edwards and Sarah Edwards) and other resources address the unique perks and challenges of working from home. The same principles of accessibility and accommodation that govern traditional home-based living apply to home-based working as well.

Meanwhile, people also have their unpaid work. Although the word "hobbies" seems somewhat dated, reminiscent of tatting lace or building model ships, that's not really fair. Hobbies, which are unpaid (and untaxed) personal pursuits, are excellent sources of mastery, self-expression, relaxation and pleasure. They keep people going mentally, physically, emotionally and often socially.

Look at the home in terms of how it supports the active pursuit of hobbies. Can space be allocated for the hobby, with strong lighting and accessible storage? Is there a sturdy, wheelchair-accessible table or workbench? Can equipment be stored locally and used safely? Are safety precautions observed for using power tools and chemicals, such as paints and solvents?

Here are some scenarios: For the serious reader, is there a good supportive chair with a task lamp? For the music lover, how accessible are the controls for the stereo system, and can it be heard well without waking the neighbors? For the movie buff, how are the seating, lighting and sightlines for the home theater? For puzzle mavens, is there a good strong task light over a sturdy card or bridge table with a removable puzzle surface?

Supporting the development of hobbies reminds people that there's more to being home all day than eating, sleeping and taking pills (or even working). Home life should be balanced and enriching, not just a way of passing the time before bowing to the inevitable.

Just a Butterfly: Social Interaction

There's mounting evidence that social interaction may support healthy mental aging, and that social interaction plus mental engagement may work even better, such as through social, memory-intensive games like bridge.

Grooming, gossiping, growing old together—these time-less activities may help us age more gracefully.

That's not surprising. If the human brain thrives on something new, then other people are the best of novelties, the most stimulating of all social and intellectual stimuli.

Isolation is the enemy of social stimulation, with dully predictable results. For example, one Swedish study found that more outgoing, relaxed people had a lower risk of developing Alzheimer's disease. Other studies have suggested that loneliness and shrunken social networks also raise the odds of cognitive decline.

Still, in old age, friends fall away; disability and ill-ness start to limit mobility and communication. Even sociable people find it harder to have steady social contact. Thus, it becomes important to periodically review and revise how people socialize and entertain, to ensure that changing abilities don't limit community involvement.

Simplifying meals and adjusting expectations may make it easier to keep 'em coming. For example, shifting invites from dinner to brunch allows guests to drive during daylight hours. Potlucks allow everyone to contribute and lighten the host's burden.

Older people tend to stick loyally to routines. It may be easier for them to establish and maintain traditions, especially those that are easy to uphold, such as home-based weekly pizza nights, Sunday movie matinees, game days and more. Large-type cookbooks with simple recipes that respect special dietary needs may further extend the ability to socialize.

Welcome to Scam-a-Lot: Fighting Fraud

People aging at home have to contend with yet another mental challenge, the fight against scammers. Research contradicts the stereotype of lonely old widows falling prey to scammers, revealing instead that middle-aged men with money are actually more likely to be lured into financial traps.

Even so, older people are popular targets. They tend to have significant assets to draw on, may not have the savvy to understand telemarketing/Internet scams, and frequently live alone, making them eager to interact with people who seem to care about them.

In addition, cognitive impairment (whatever the source or age) can make people more vulnerable to scams. When people have a problem with memory, confusion or poor judgment, others can and will take advantage.

Even in normal, healthy aging, the mind changes in such a way that makes it harder to tell fact from fiction. People may remember incorrectly or not at all, allowing a scam artist to say, "You forgot to pay me" (when they did), or "The estimate was $500" (when it was $400). To counter the power of suggestion, get everything from estimates to receipts in writing.

Just hang up. It's okay to hang up. That's what fraud experts tell people who have a hard time with telemarketers. Although it may go against the good manners of many older people, it is not rude to cut off a call with someone who has come in uninvited by the phone line, the same way it is not rude to shut the door against uninvited visitors.

Telemarketers, whether they sound nice or nasty, have one and only one goal in mind: To get a commitment, most likely financial. They are not out to do anybody any favors. They are grifters with gadgets, looking for cash.

My personal philosophy: If I want a good deal, I'll look for it. Remember the old adage? If it sounds too good to be true, it probably is.

Similarly, it's important for older people using the Internet to be trained to detect computer viruses, worms, spyware, Trojan horses, email spam and other digital misdeeds. Keep anti-everything software up-to-date and discuss privacy protections for the use of social media. It's important for people of any age to understand computer security. Organizations such as SeniorNet and Net Literacy's Senior Connects program help people safely cross the digital divide.

My canny father-in-law has his own little fraud-proofing trick. As an older person living in a retirement area, he's all too aware that he's a magnet for scam artists. To stave them off, he refuses to do anything over the phone or by mail and insists that anybody trying to sell him anything see him in person. What's more, he won't see a representative. He asks to meet the principal.

He reasons that if people really want the business, they'll show up. And what a surprise, nobody does! His strategy has weeded out the hustlers and helped him feel he has some kind of quality control. At the same time, it gracefully obscures the fact that he had to give up driving.

In the rare event that someone does offer to meet in person, be wary of giving a home address or meeting at home. It remains far more personally secure to meet a new person in a public place. An older person can also check with the Better Business Bureau, ask someone to investigate or send a representative to check things out.

Another kind of scammer is only too happy to come to the door. In fact, that's how they work. These are the contractors who show up out of the blue when the weather gets nice and say they're working in your neighborhood and have "extra material" left over. Their high-pressure tactics include pointing out a "problem" you didn't see before, offering a "free" inspection (and breaking something on purpose so they can fix it), and demanding full (in cash) payment up front.

Among their many fix-it "talents" are duct cleaning, driveway sealant, leaky foundations, landscaping, furnace and roofing repair. So beware. Check identification, licensing and permits, and references, and get multiple bids. If something were really that urgent, you probably would have known about it. Learn more about preventing home-repair scams in Chapter 8.

Meanwhile, what to do about those crooks that come to the door pretending to be utility or cable company workers? They may seem to wear proper uniforms with (fake) IDs or badges, but they're only playing a part. Energy resellers also send aggressive salespeople door to door to hustle new business in sometimes misleading ways.

Older people, like anyone else, should refuse access to anyone arriving unannounced. If there is any doubt or concern about home safety or service interruptions, call the utility directly and ask if anyone was sent.

Finally, keep that fixed income fixed. It is essential to keep sensitive information with account numbers and passwords out of sight, as well as checkbooks out of reach of casual visitors. *Never* give out Social Security or Social Insurance numbers or date of birth over the phone or online unless you are 100 percent sure you trust the person you are dealing with.

Always shred personal documents, especially bills, notices, and anything containing bank account, credit card, social insurance numbers and the like. Tear up the rest of the personal mail. For people without shredders, or who have difficulty using them, local police departments sometimes offer free shredding events (which, in turn, help them to prevent white-collar crime such as identity theft). Paid shredding services will come to the home. For additional information, see the Appendix.

A Bitter Pill: Medication Management

Aging at home brings another mind-body challenge: Kitchen counters that are starting to look more like a shelf at the local drugstore. Many older individuals take five or more prescription drugs a day, a situation that, beyond the potential for medical complications, creates special challenges for both storage and memory.

Starting with storage, a warm, moist environment isn't the best place to store medications. Keep them out of the bathroom in a cool, dry place. Next, place a magnifying glass near prescription bottles to help with reading the small print on the labels. Some pharmacies can print larger prescription labels using bigger fonts to enable easier reading; ask about this option. Visually impaired patients can use tactile objects or materials like felt to help identify medications and convey basic instructions such as doses per day.

To keep track of daily medications, post a list with names, doses, times and any special instructions (with/without food, etc.) inside a kitchen cabinet, on the refrigerator, or wherever pills are stored. Because medicine regimens change, an erasable whiteboard or chalkboard calendar, or an easily updated, computer-generated template or blank chart, may be in order.

Take the list of medications to health-care providers on each visit to keep them up to date on all your medicines, vitamins and supplements.

Research has found that working out a paper-and-pencil medicine schedule with a health-care professional increases a patient's ability to follow instructions, so try to arrange a session to go over the routine with a doctor, nurse or pharmacist.

When medicines are taken for ongoing, chronic conditions, they can be set up for months at a time with the use of electronic pillboxes and automatic medication dispensers. Some can even be monitored by caregivers (see the Appendix for resources).

These special pillboxes and dispensers can be programmed to help people take their medicines in the right amounts, the right way, at the right times. For example, when someone opens a compartment of an electronic pillbox, a time stamp is sent to caregivers by the phone line.

Assistive technology can take things a step further. For example, alarm clocks, gadget-based alarms, or special vibrating watches can be set to go off when it's time to take medicines.

Periodically, go through medicine bottles to discard anything old and out of date. Keep only the most recent bottles to avoid confusion and stockpiles of old drugs. Periodically check for and discard out-of-date over-the-counter (OTC) drugs as well.

Finally, is the medicine cabinet too small or out of reach? Try storing items in an old-fashioned shoe bag with clear plastic pockets, or a special travel toiletry bag, either of which can hang on a sturdy hook on the back of a bedroom or pantry door, or on a wall hook in the kitchen.

In the bathroom itself, by the way, cluster grooming items to spare memory and minimize bending and reaching. Store extra sets of underclothes in the bathroom to help people refresh themselves if necessary.

Live Long and Perspire: Fitness At Home

Many people ask about the best mental exercise. Is it crossword puzzles? Computer games? They're fine if you enjoy them, but don't expect miracles.

The best mental exercise is physical. First, it feels great right way. That's the biggest plus, which keeps folks coming back for more. Second, studies show that older people who take an active role in maintaining their strength, stamina and flexibility simply age better—and that includes their minds.

Their mental functions test better. They're more able to do what they want without pain or limitations. They're healthier, more independent, and less susceptible to the "lifestyle diseases," such as heart disease, diabetes, and some cancers that afflict so many sedentary older people. They live longer. They even stay out of nursing homes longer.

As Jane Brody, *The New York Times* personal-health columnist, wrote, "Regular exercise is the only well-established fountain of youth, and it's free." Alzheimer's specialists and exercise pros share a common refrain: What's good for the heart is good for the brain. Indeed, researchers are excited about early evidence that regular exercise not only indirectly boosts brain power by curbing cardiovascular disease but also directly pumps up key parts of the brain itself.

In any case, taking it easy doesn't make for easy aging. As the late fitness great Jack LaLanne observed, "People don't die of old age; they die of inactivity." Regular exercise helps to reduce blood pressure and blood sugar, manage cholesterol, strengthen bones, improve posture and circulation, build lung capacity, and strengthen the heart and other muscles. It helps people keep their balance, which helps prevent falls. It "oils" the joints, easing the pain of arthritis. A regular fitness program also helps people relax, stave off depression and sleep better.

It's not about weight loss. For that, alas, you still have to eat less (and also exercise). It's about everything else.

The benefits apply to everyone, not just lifelong jocks. That's because genes hold less power over our health as we age, making "lifestyle factors," such as diet and exercise much more important. After middle age, the evidence for the benefits of exercise is striking.

So it's never too late to start. Even moderate levels of exercise can make a big difference both in how you feel today and in your long-term health. If you or your parents are more everyday athletes than Olympian elite, that's just fine.

Still, why can it be hard to exercise? The reasons are many. Time is always a factor, though we hope it's more available after the kids are grown. Inexperience is another factor, although it can be overcome. But attitudes get in the way.

Many older people grew up in a time when conscious, structured exercise was not hip or even encouraged. They grew up on Frank Sinatra crooning, "Let's Take It Nice and Easy," not Olivia Newton-John shrieking, "Let's Get Physical." Intense physical activity reminded them of blue-collar life as dockworkers and ditch diggers, miners and machinists. Today's oldest generation was thrilled to climb out of the ditches and settle into the comfy white-collar chairs of middle management.

Meanwhile, women were once told that they don't sweat; they "mist" and they "glow." They were supposed to be slender, not bulky.

And the fitness industry itself has not kept pace with demographics. For decades, commercial gyms have marketed themselves as places to get "ripped" and "cut," with lots of high-intensity aerobics classes, thumping disco music, and images of gleaming young muscles. Many gyms are starting to figure out how to accommodate older people, but off-putting images linger in promotional materials.

In a group setting, water aerobics, fitness classes or dance tailored to the needs of older people may be more suitable. Look for instructors certified to teach this age group.

The bottom line is that inactive older people may feel flummoxed about exercise for a reason. It doesn't mean that you or they don't want to. It only means that as with any change in behavior, it's not going to be as simple as going from Point A to Point B. There are lots of little steps in between.

Thus, any good exercise program should start in the body part between the ears. Before even putting on a pair of sweats, think it through and talk it out. Figure out what stands in the way of a regular fitness routine and what can be done about those barriers. Changing behavior is rarely an overnight process, so allow yourself or the people you hope will become more active to contemplate change first.

The next step is to set specific, achievable and measurable fitness goals, exploring what works best for the person and situation, structuring schedules and the environment to be as supportive as possible, and learning the basics of safe, effective exercise. With time and attention, it's all quite doable.

Face facts: "You're going to get hurt if you exercise, but you'll get also hurt if you *don't* exercise, and you'll be more resilient if you've built up the muscles," a doctor told a friend of mine who lifts weights in her 70s. Focusing on the benefits of regular exercise appears to be a lot more motivating than focusing on the consequences of inaction, so positive goals are more likely to meet with success.

Because staying fit is such an important contributor to healthy and independent aging, the rest of this chapter will cover some basics and offer tips on using one's home to stay fit. Additional resources are listed in the Appendix. One caution: Anyone over the age of 50, regardless of medical condition, should talk to a doctor before starting an exercise program.

Primary Care: The Components of Fitness

Fitness begins with four primary components and their roles in active, independent aging.

1. *Cardiovascular or cardiorespiratory fitness* builds the heart, lungs and circulation. Aerobic and anaerobic (depending on the use of oxygen) conditioning allows the heart to pump more efficiently, the lungs to move more oxygen, and the circulatory system to better reach every part of the body with essential nutrients. "Cardio" workouts help manage or even prevent high blood sugar and reduce the rates of heart disease and stroke. Their power to help people feel happy and energetic, and sleep better at night, is truly motivating.

Cardiovascular exercise has its own internal rhythms that include a warm-up period, a lengthier period of peak demands on the heart and lungs (when you sweat the most), and a gradual cool-down and recovery. With age, the warm-up and recovery periods become more critical. No one should undertake high-intensity exercise without adjusting for age, resting heart rate and medical condition. Music sets the pace for people as they move through the various intensity levels of cardiovascular exercise. Scientists think that music aids exercise in part because it distracts people from discomfort while encouraging them to work harder.

2. *Muscle conditioning* builds stronger muscles, raises the metabolism, helps people carry out daily activities better, reduces the chance of injury, and improves balance to reduce the risk of falls. It seems to help improve bone density and even improves heart health. Muscle conditioning also reduces the pain and stiffness of arthritis by building the muscles that support key joints.

Sounds amazing, right? So why don't more people lift weights? Perhaps because of competitive bodybuilding, lifting weights may be perceived to be hard, dangerous or ridiculous. Women in particular are wary of looking unfeminine despite the fact that their female hormones will keep them from bulking up.

Depending on body type and the intensity of the work (weight and frequency), an older person can pump iron and look anything from nicely toned to Mrs. Universe. Going low and slow can work very well for older people.

Curious (and I hope you are)? Experienced, certified personal trainer or fitness instructors trained in the special needs of older adults can set up safe and suitable muscle-conditioning programs. Illustrated how-to books are listed in the Appendix.

3. *Flexibility* exercises stretch the muscles after all those strength-building contractions. They restore them to a soft and supple condition, allowing muscles to heal and rebuild. Flexibility also helps people function better, with less stiffness and soreness.

Dynamic movements that take joints through their full range of motion help people limber up and reduce stiffness. In addition, even static (holding in place) post-workout stretching feels good, helps prevent muscle and joint injury, allows your heart to cool down, and aids relaxation. Stretching feels good. It's a wonderful reward for all that effort. Always warm up before stretching; never stretch cold muscles or they will tense, making them more prone to injury.

Yoga is very popular now, but bear in mind that it emphasizes only some aspects of fitness. It has a place in a balanced fitness program, but certain postures may aggravate back or other musculoskeletal problems. People with osteoporosis must avoid twisting and flexing the spine. Don't hold positions for too long, and don't do anything that hurts. Consult a doctor and/or a fitness professional certified to work with older adults before embarking on any such exercise.

4. *Body composition*—or the relative proportions of lean mass, fat mass, body water and bone mass that make

up our body weight—is the final primary fitness component. Proper exercise and diet can help people maintain these components in healthy ratios to one another. Beyond cardiovascular fitness, muscle conditioning, flexibility and body composition, secondary aspects of fitness include:

✦ Balance, the ability to restore equilibrium;
✦ Agility, the ability to change direction quickly;
✦ Coordination, the ability to organize one's movements effectively.

Other secondary components of obvious value in aging include reaction time and the mental capacity for planned movement.

As you might imagine, balance becomes especially important with age, when people become prone to dizziness and falls (see Chapter 2). The best exercise programs for older adults will incorporate balance work, as part of or in addition to the flexibility/cool-down phase of a class or a workout. Tai chi has been found to aid balance and is endorsed by doctors who treat older people.

Finally, cross-training isn't just for Olympians. Everyday athletes need to mix up their exercise routines in order to train different parts of the body and reduce the impact of repetitive stress on specific joints and muscles.

Silver Sneakers: Fitness Over 50
First, it's essential to ask a doctor before starting any exercise program, even yoga. A cardiac stress test may

be in order, or there might be a chat about arthritis or bone density. There are special considerations for people who have high blood pressure or strokes, as well as for people with heart trouble, diabetes, Parkinson's disease and other chronic ailments.

Safe, effective and enjoyable exercise programs must take individual needs into account. It's frustrating to start, overdo or do the wrong thing, get hurt, wait to recover, and start over. A thoughtfully designed program will help even the newest fitness buff to stay on an even track.

The U.S. Centers for Disease Control and Prevention recommend that adults get at least 30 minutes of moderate exercise at least five days a week, including walking, cycling and gardening. What's more, that time can be divided into shorter sessions, such as two 15-minute or three 10-minute walks.

More intense and prolonged aerobic activity will further promote health, but measurable benefits have been obtained in as little as half an hour a day.

For people who enjoy more vigorous and intense aerobic activity, such as jogging or running, an hour and a quarter (half the time for moderate activity) will do. Or mix it up.

Organizations like the American Heart Association and American College of Sports Medicine offer more specific guidelines. They say moderate exercise could mean brisk walking at the rate of at least 4 miles an hour, ballroom dancing, or playing doubles tennis. Vigorous exercise could mean jogging or running at the pace of at least 4.5 miles an hour, playing basketball or singles tennis, or biking at the speed of more than 12 miles an hour.

Maximum benefit comes from enjoying cardiorespiratory exercise *four to seven days a week*, flexibility and balance exercises *daily*, and muscle conditioning *two to four days a week*.

Muscle-strengthening activities for all major muscle groups (legs, hips, back, abdomen, shoulders, chest and arms) should be performed with days off in between to allow the muscles to repair and renew themselves.

Slowly increase the duration and intensity of exercise. Higher intensity exercise goes quicker but is harder on the joints. It also still requires appropriate warm up and recovery.

Scheduling helps, best done when reviewing the overall calendar and daily routine. Write the plan directly on the daily calendar like a doctor's appointment or lunch with a friend, allowing time to change clothes and wash up.

For example, block in 30 minutes for cardio, 15 minutes for lifting weights, and 10 minutes for stretching. Rotating work with weights among different parts of the body can allow busy people to get everything in, as muscles need a recovery day between sessions.

Consider alternating days of upper- or lower-body work. That's easy to remember and gives you something to do every day. Set watches, alarm clocks or computers with reminders for upcoming sessions.

Where does exercise happen? About 40 percent of Americans like to work out in groups. They go to the gym, or join running, cycling or swimming clubs. Good for them, especially if they can cross-train, balance their fitness routines and avoid injury.

What about the other 60 percent of people who don't exercise in group settings or join teams? Sometimes informal groups that meet less often can share information and boost commitment. Many people cycle in and out of group activities as a way to jump-start exercise after being inactive, learn new things from new instructors or recover from an illness or injury. Some people use group instruction or personal training as a cost-effective way to learn how to do it themselves. Others read books (see the Appendix for recommendations) or watch exercise videos, DVDs or YouTube segments. And much of this happens at home.

Pump It Up: The Home Gym

Dedicated space for exercise increases the odds of actual exercise. A home gym, whether in a separate room or a clearly demarked portion of a room, is a big visible cue to get moving. A home exercise space also makes it easier to work out when the weather is bad or it's hard to get to the gym, and enables a personal trainer to come to the house as well.

An exercise space should support the primary components of fitness. For cardiovascular fitness, that may mean accommodating large items such as treadmills, stationary bikes (regular or incumbent, the latter of which takes some stress off the lower back), stair steppers or stair climbers, or elliptical machines (see the Appendix for fitness resources). Make sure to have enough electrical outlets for this equipment. Also, realize it's too easy to just "ride" these exercise machines without doing much for the heart. Try not to treat them like loungers.

For those who are fit enough and whose knees actually work, simple activities such as jumping rope can take place on resilient, shock-absorbent matting, always in supportive athletic shoes. Others with strong leg muscles and joints may use the kinds of nonslip steps used in aerobics classes. Cushioned, secure matting or resilient flooring can also be used with exercise videos and dance-type routines, even with home videogame consoles that offer exercise programs and dance-type routines.

To support home athletes musically, the more tech savvy might enjoy setting up iPod playlists and burning CDs with someone's favorite tunes, including ample warm-up and recovery periods.

Muscle conditioning doesn't require big, fancy weight machines. In fact, those aren't always suitable for people of smaller-than-average size, especially women, and the use of tension resistance doesn't put as much beneficial stress on the ends of the bones.

Simple hand, or free, weights are more versatile and build bone better because they work against the body itself. Buy them inexpensively at gym supply, sporting goods and some discount stores, and store them on a special rack or in an elevated plastic crate.

Always buy hand weights in pairs. Rubberized coatings cost a little more but offer a superior grip. Uncoated cast-iron dumbbells are very durable, but the finish tends to flake off (kind of like I do between hamstring curls). It comes down to personal preference.

An older adult's program may find a previously inactive person lifting weights anywhere from 1 to 3 pounds for smaller muscles and up to 5 to 10 pounds for larger muscles. (How do you know how heavy? If you or your loved one can perform 8 to 10 repetitions of an exercise comfortably with control, that's a good starting level.) Specialized tools such as push-up bars or disks (ask in fitness equipment stores) can make the push-up, an essential upper-body exercise, easier on the hands and arms.

Hand grips and pliable balls help build hand strength. Keep a basket of these "toys" by the TV chair or sofa.

For the lower body, weighted ankle circlets (they look like doughnuts) are a good starting point for beginners. As leg muscles develop, people can move up to heavier strap-on weights that fasten with Velcro straps and have removable lead slugs to adjust the resistance.

Only in rare circumstances should anyone strap or hang weights on joints that will be in motion. Ankle weights throw people off balance and are not suitable for walking.

Many older people like to use resistance bands and tubes, which are light and inexpensive and come in different lengths, levels of resistance and with or without handles. Often used in rehabilitation, they have their uses and limitations, requiring training for effective use. Stability balls and balance platforms are often used to augment exercise as well.

Given the space, it's great to have a weight bench, even without a barbell frame. Make sure it is stable and wide enough to support the user securely when he or she lies down, both front and back. And something as low-tech as a door frame can help exercisers stretch the chest and arms.

Sturdy chairs can be used for working with hand weights; for working the triceps (push yourself up, sit down, repeat); for certain stretches, such as a standing hamstring or quadriceps stretch; or for extra stability while doing squats, an essential lower-body exercise.

Flexibility work calls for a comfortable nonslip exercise or yoga mat that folds or rolls up for easy storage.

At least one large mirror is essential for checking form, especially while lifting weights. Many people avoid mirrors as they age, but really, especially if you're exercising, be proud of your effort.

Home gyms should have a stable surface for a water bottle. The body needs water before, during and after exercise. Also make space for instructions, towels, adequate ventilation, and maybe a fan. Finally, a radio, CD player and/or iPod dock can provide musical pacing and motivation for workouts.

Bits and Pieces: Working Out Whenever

Not all exercise has to be structured into formal sessions. In fact, one of the benefits of having more time is being able to work activity into the routines of daily life. In the long run, good healthy habits may be more beneficial than a gym membership.

The key is to see regular exercise as a part of daily life, like eating and brushing one's teeth.

Other than that, there's no one right way to get exercise. The key is to be flexible. Fitness planning can change according to personal preference, physical condition, local facilities, social support, budget, even the seasons. Here are some additional tips for working in fitness year-round:

+ Keep a log of fitness activities to chart improvement and write down fitness goals.
+ Develop cross-generational fitness programs to make it a family affair.
+ Review course catalogs from local schools, gyms and community centers, and sign up for the next season's fitness or swimming class. Every January 1, plan the fitness year.
+ Make a list of all the sports or activities you or your loved ones have always wanted to try and brainstorm how to fit them into the coming year.
+ Use a Web-based or smartphone application to track progress, as well as for reminders that it's time to exercise.
+ Ask a friend to be your fitness buddy, to talk out your program and check in. Offer to reciprocate. Accountability and structure will make exercise a habit.
+ Designate a handy, accessible place to store fitness gear and other equipment. Keep more than

one set of clothes for the gym, so there's always something clean.

◆ Have written exercise plans for bad-weather days when it's not possible to get to the gym or class. All-or-nothing thinking has no place in fitness. Whatever is done will be good.

◆ Discuss with a doctor, physical therapist, certified personal trainer, or other qualified professional how to exercise after recovering from surgery or a prolonged illness. Stuff happens. Prepare yourself mentally and emotionally to deal with life's setbacks.

◆ If it's not possible to do what was done before, celebrate and develop what can be done now.

◆ Those who (like me) have benefited from the services of a licensed physical therapist or phys-iotherapist should keep the illustrated exercise sheets in a three-ring binder. Due to the injury that got you there in the first place, you may have a weak joint or muscle group and will benefit from doing those prescribed exercises in the future. Keep expert advice handy and organized. Talk to your doctor and therapist.

Beyond that, there are many things that you can do around the house to build and maintain fitness. Here are some recommended activities that build informal exercise into daily life, grouped by the primary components of fitness.

Cardiovascular Fitness

✦ Walk to a friend's house and back for a meal. Bend your arms and keep them at or above chest height for a much better cardio workout. You'll feel the difference!

✦ In nice weather, walk after dinner, maybe with grandchildren and/or a dog. Try for a pace faster than a leisurely stroll. You should be comfortably winded and still able to talk.

✦ Clean the kitchen shelves and wash the kitchen floor. Wiping builds shoulder muscles; sweeping and mopping are totally cardio!

✦ Walk to the grocery store and carry home the bags (stand straight, shoulders back), or use a rolling cart, depending on the load, your strength and ground conditions.

✦ Work in the yard. Skip the leaf-blower and use a rake. The neighbors will be grateful for the quiet.

✦ Call friends to set up a regular walking program at the mall in the winter and through the neighborhood in nicer seasons. Social interaction is amazingly helpful for both mind and body.

✦ Walk up and down the stairs. If balance is good, build leg strength by skipping the handrail going up (or loosely gliding the hand over it). *Always use the handrail going down.*

Muscle Conditioning

✦ Hide the remote control, and make yourself get up more.

✦ Rise from chairs without leaning on the arms or back.

✦ Stop the plop! Sit down slowly with control.

✦ Go up the stairs without leaning on the handrail.

✦ Use hand and ankle weights while watching TV, including hand grips.

✦ In the kitchen, do push-ups off the counter or the wall.

✦ Don't lean straight over (it hurts the spine); squat instead (builds key muscles).

✦ To build calf muscles, bounce up and down on the toes.

✦ After a 10-minute warm-up, such as a short session on the treadmill or a walk to the local mailbox, use a sturdy chair to do lower-body squats.

Flexibility and Balance

✦ After checking with the doctor, warm up and follow an easy yoga or stretching program on TV or DVD. In general, don't do anything that hurts. "No pain, no gain" is an outdated notion.

✦ Once the muscles are warm, perform stretches using the wall or sturdy chair for support, or use a nonslip floor mat while watching TV or listening to music. Hold stretches for at least 20 seconds to allow the muscle fibers to relax. In particular, learn a few different ways to stretch the hamstring muscles at the back of the thigh. Hamstrings can easily become tight, which can lead to lower back pain.

✦ While brushing your teeth, improve balance by standing with one foot in front of the other (both on the ground) or with your feet closer together. Use the vanity or wall for support as needed. Standing on one foot, a common balance exercise, can be hard for some older people.

✦ Walk heel to toe for five minutes, up and down the hallway or the living room.

Sitting Pretty? The Bottom Line

Finally, we bring you some depressingly bad news from the world of science. The newest research describes how harmful it is to just sit. That's right. Being sedentary is, all by itself, a health risk even exercise can't fix. Sweating for an hour in the morning won't make up for five hours of sitting at night.

In one large study, middle-aged men were twice as likely to have a heart attack or other cardiac event if they sat as little as two hours a day in front of a screen compared to those who sat less. Those who spent four or more hours of recreational time in front of a screen were 50 percent more likely to die of any cause. With Americans spending three to four hours a day watching TV alone, that's a problem. Premature and sudden death is surely undesirable. So are the years of chronic disease and disability that can precede a final decline.

Just how sitting leads independently to poor health is under investigation, but here's the key for anyone tempted to sit in front of the TV or computer for long periods. Once in a while, get up and move. Stop the movie every half hour and walk around a bit. By all means watch the game, but take a seventh-inning stretch in every inning. Even these minibreaks may help to short-circuit the biological damage caused by sitting still.

Given all the mental and physical challenges that lie ahead for older adults, can the dream retirement still mean a peaceful sit-down on the front porch? Perhaps, but not for hours at a time, and only after a good workout.

That's why Marilyn and Joe, our friends from the beginning of this chapter, took her memory and mood changes as a wake-up call. They took a brisk half-hour walk every day, rain or shine (rainy days at the mall), and found it an enjoyable way to reminisce and gossip.

Marilyn took up the challenge of learning a new language and signed up for tai chi classes to bolster her balance, while Joe bought a second-hand weight bench and some hand weights for the den. After three sessions of advice from a personal trainer certified to work with older adults, Joe lifts weights three times a week while the news is on. Marilyn is thinking of trying it herself. Linking exercise to a regular habit makes it easy to succeed. Now they both have more staying power than they did before her surgery.

LET'S GET STARTED
Top Tips for a Holistic Home

_____ Learn about normal brain aging and try to relax about normal changes (stress and anxiety hurt memory!).

_____ Schedule one week to notice the information that slips through the cracks and develop systems to fill the gap, such as ready-made shopping lists and the use of timers and reminders.

_____ Review organizing and scheduling systems to better suit current needs and capabilities.

_____ Schedule a week to develop a detailed exercise program with SMART goals: specific, measurable, attainable, realistic and timely.

_____ Learn age-specific target heart rates for different activity levels.

_____ Hire a personal trainer to assess fitness, and develop a six-week start-up package. It takes a certain number of weeks to make something a habit.

_____ Don't make it too easy to sit: Hide the remote, remove the cushions, consider a standing desk and take regular movement breaks.

LET'S GO SHOPPING

Top Tools for a Holistic Home

Mind

- ☐ Holders for reading glasses
- ☐ Custom-made shopping lists
- ☐ Alarm watches (preferably easy to set)
- ☐ Timers with loud buzzers and ringers
- ☐ Medication lists and pill organizers
- ☐ Small notebooks for on-the-go notes and referrals
- ☐ Clothing with pockets
- ☐ Organizing handbooks
- ☐ Label-making machine (not just for file folders)
- ☐ Accessible shelving, hooks, cabinets, cubbies
- ☐ Camera for taking pictures of cabinet and box contents
- ☐ Hobby-related materials and storage
- ☐ Large-print cookbooks

Body

- ☐ Heart-rate monitor watch
- ☐ Pedometer (increase steps per day from baseline)
- ☐ Hand weights
- ☐ Exercise/yoga mat
- ☐ Cardiovascular exercise equipment (treadmill, recumbent bike, etc.)

- ☐ Stress-reduction balls to squeeze and spring-loaded grips to build hand strength
- ☐ Ankle weights
- ☐ Wall-mounted mirror
- ☐ Exercise clothes and proper footwear (get two pairs and alternate; active exercisers replace their athletic shoes about twice a year to get better support and avoid injury)
- ☐ Motivating music and energizing images (of yourself in your best shape, whenever that was)
- ☐ Rolling grocery cart (for grocery and mall trips to increase walking and reduce dependence on the car)

Chapter 7
The Useful Home: Supportive Surroundings

Teresa likes her house and wants to stay there, but she feels as if it's twice as big as it used to be. She always took care of the inside and her late husband, Anthony, handled the outside. In fact, his messy workbench was off limits, but between them, they managed to have staying power. Now that he's gone, her to-do list includes the yard, the garage and all kinds of maintenance. Frankly, she's a little overwhelmed.

"Home, sweet home" doesn't exactly call to mind the laundry room. But any home, whether an apartment with a garbage chute down the hall or a suburban colonial with a stuffed two-car garage, has a range of utility areas and surroundings that, together, contribute to or detract from an older person's quality of life. These spaces deserve the same kind of attention as the living room, kitchen and washrooms. So grab a clipboard and a pen. It's time for a home inspection.

Welcome Mat: Outside the House

Start with the approach. Are the house, unit or apartment numbers clearly visible from the street or hallway, and well lit at night? This is important for both visitors and emergency personnel.

Next, can residents safely and easily reach the mailbox? If a community mailbox is now too high because its owner has lost height or sits in a wheelchair, can it be switched with the mailbox of someone taller?

Outdoor matting should be large, heavy, skid-proof and secure with a rough enough texture to remove most debris from footwear before it gets into the house. Boot scrapers are great for this.

Entrance stairs should have rock-solid handrails on each side, with steps in working order and no loose boards or stones. Consider rubber mats or runners on steps, especially during slippery times of year, and shake them clear daily.

Are the walkways to or around the home free of clutter? Repair holes, wide cracks and loose bricks; correct uneven areas in pathways. If you need concrete poured, ask the contractors to use a special gritty additive to increase traction. Walkers should avoid stepping on painted concrete or asphalt when it's wet. As yours truly learned the hard way in a parking lot, those cheery yellow lines have a slippery dark side.

To help protect those who live in a multi-unit property, bear in mind that owners are concerned about lawsuits. Perhaps a quiet discussion with or a note to management about the needs of older residents could result in improved maintenance and better lighting, inside and out.

In a four-season climate, have sensible plans and procedures in place to remove fallen leaves (especially when wet), snow and ice. In some cases, it may mean a simple check of rakes and shovels to ensure they're accessible, well maintained and easy to manage. In others, it may mean hiring a lawn or shoveling service. Place prefilled small buckets of sand or kitty litter, and smaller, easier-to-lift bags of rock salt next to the front door or just inside. New warming mats that plug into outdoor receptacles have embedded heating coils that help melt walkway ice.

Entry Points: Doors and Floors

Improve entryways with lighted doorbells and wide-angle peepholes. Peepholes can also be installed at wheelchair height. Some doors have sidelights that offer a view of visitors. Intercoms can also allow residents to communicate with visitors from a convenient point.

To automate outdoor lighting, install photo-sensitive porch or entryway lighting that comes on at dusk and goes off at dawn. Motion-sensor lights around the house perimeter help people as they approach the front door in the dark as much as they deter burglars. Security cameras add extra security.

If the front door is currently unsheltered, can you add an awning or enclosure to provide some shelter from the storm? Is there a small weatherproof table or chair to hold parcels and shopping bags at a back-friendly height while someone fumbles with the keys?

Lever-type door handles are easier than knobs for someone with arthritis or limited hand strength to operate. Some screen/storm doors have foot-operated buttons to prop them open. Grillwork on glass storm doors and stick-on decals on sliding glass patio doors can make them easier to see, as can contrasting framing. Come to think of it, a bright or vivid front-door color will make it easier to see as well. It's especially important to have the lock area stand out, to the eyes and to the touch.

Remember that older eyes find it harder to adjust to changing light conditions, so ensure that overhead entryway lighting is even and not glaringly bright.

Just as with indoor rooms, assess the flooring threshold from outside to inside to see whether it can be bevelled or smoothed. The goal is a step-free entrance from the driveway, sidewalk or other approach to the main floor or central living area.

Inside the front door, in a closet or a cordoned-off area (see Chapter 2), provide footwear for poor weather. Pull-on traction cleats or spikes that fit over the soles of boots and shoes can help prevent falls in ice and snow. Are there wet boots and shoes? Please do not throw towels on the floor. That creates a serious hazard. Instead, stash a spare rubber-backed bathmat or plastic boot tray near the entrance.

Outer Space: Property Management

Check how Mother Nature is aging as well. Inspect trees and shrubs for signs of rot or broken, bent limbs that should be removed before they fall. Trim shrubs so they don't crowd or block walkways. Stormy weather can strew hazards all around a house.

It (almost) goes without saying that deck and patio surfaces should be clean and clear, with well-constructed handrails on both sides of any steps and a secure railing all around. Deck and porch steps can be painted in bright, contrasting colors. Use outdoor no-skid tape to edge the bannisters.

Amateur gardeners may find that container gardens and raised potting beds are much easier on the knees and back, with plantings no less wonderful to view.

Pools are the number-one cause of backyard deaths. If the pool is no longer being used, drain it, and close it off with an easy-to-see cover. If necessary, add an additional locked safety fence. Local regulations must be met or exceeded.

Work areas (including laundry rooms) need to be clean, well lit and ventilated, containing a phone and a list of emergency numbers. Laundry could be easier with front-loading machines, especially if moved to ground or bedroom level.

In general, give some thought to cleaning. It's hard on older eyes, arthritic joints and achy backs.

Lighter vacuums or whole-house vacuum systems, long-handled dusters, simpler furniture and fixtures, and reduced clutter can lower maintenance demands. Also consider a gift of regular cleaning and maintenance services.

It's also high time for a domestic goddess, some Einstein of the Everyday, to figure out a way to make it easier to make the beds and use the closets, the latter perhaps through open, mid-height shelving and lower hanging-rods.

In the garage, apply the same storage guidelines used inside the house. Clear the floor and move heavily used items to lower shelves or wall hooks. Improve the lighting to provide even coverage and fewer shadows, especially in corners, which tend to fill up quickly. Use kitty litter or sand to soak up any oil spills, and store flammable materials away from any source of heat or flame. Clearly mark all chemicals.

For residents lucky enough to have garages that lead right into the house, these passageways are often overlooked. Using the guidance of Chapter 2, check and improve floor thresholds, lighting and handrails, as well as any stairs.

Higher Ground: Ups and Downs

Anyone using a ladder should never stand on the top three rungs. Center the body between rails. Don't reach to the side and push or pull on anything. Ever!

Should changing circumstances necessitate the use of an entry ramp, here are some general guidelines before you talk to your contractor. First, any ramp—even pre-fabricated—must meet regulations for the proper slope. Short, steep ramps are dangerous and hard to use. Safety codes specify that weight-bearing ramps have a 12:1 ratio. In other words, they should rise or fall by one unit of vertical space for every 12 units of horizontal space. This creates a long and very modest slope. For example, a ramp that carries weight over 8 yards (24 feet) would rise by 2 feet from start to finish.

Slopes of 1 in 15, 1 in 18, or 1 in 20 require less effort and are recommended if the primary users have limited strength or stamina, as they may be easier to use without help, according to the Canadian Mortgage and Housing Corporation, which posts information on accessible housing (see Appendix). Shallower ramps must be longer.

Before building a ramp, check any neighborhood covenants and local regulations. You can hire local carpenters or contractors to build a ramp, but make sure they follow the guidelines.

Roll 'Em: Technology *a la Cart*

Homes can be made fully accessible and accommodating, but we still have to go out and get things. Bring 'em home with the world's second greatest invention—the wheel.

Rolling carts were once scorned by the baby boomers whose mothers used those fold-up metal-wire contraptions for their supermarket shopping. Now we're coming to our senses. Instead of tacky, we see smart. Instead of "Why don't they take the car?" we say, "What fuel-saving, fitness-building efficiency!"

Those ladies raised in the Depression era knew a few things. Those carts seem to last forever. A rust spot here, a slipped joint there—it was no worse than what happened to our moms themselves.

Still, there's always room for improvement, maybe even a little style. We've starting to see more current and functional rolling carts and bags in places such as organizer stores.

Carts like that make healthy sense. They carry more weight without burdening the back and allow shoppers to walk instead of ride.

And here's another tip: Rolling backpacks, which are popular among students, make good carry-ons for all but the smallest airplanes. One caution: The wheel mechanism adds weight, a pain when the bag has to be hoisted over thresholds or on stairs. If you know you'll traverse a space without a lot of flat surface or elevators, reconsider or assign a lucky someone as a designated carrier.

Around the house, a lightweight dolly helps with moving heavier items. (One of my tricks: Load stacks of books or similar items on a thick beach towel, then gently tug to slide across the floor.) A wheelbarrow has a multitude of uses, inside and out, and there's always the little red wagon. Find one at a garage sale, and you'll never run out of uses—or children willing to help.

Pave Paradise . . . Please

To stay off-premises for a moment, give a shout out to my mother-in-law, not only because her hearing aids don't work but also because she has been an astute observer of barriers to living with disability. An early proponent of ergonomic thinking, my mother-in-law spent her life doing things like buying toy brooms because they better fit her 4-foot-10-inch height. Well into her 80s, she lives in South Florida and can't understand the current trend toward using paver stones in lieu of smooth asphalt.

At 88, you see, you don't want quaint. When you fill your prescription at Wal-Mart, you don't want neo-Victorian village. You want an even surface for your cane tip, so you don't wobble and go down. You don't want your heels to catch in those cute little crevices.

And what if you have a walker? Like my father-in-law, you might unhappily reroute yourself through the busy parking lot because you can't push the walker over that bumpy sidewalk. What's next for these good people, the servants' entrance?

So, when it comes to paving paradise, let's hope developers consider their ultimate customers and find alternative designs and materials. Perhaps when shopping centers, residential developments and recreational facilities find that *nouveau-oldeau* is turning off their customers, things will change.

And what's with the trend toward open, uncovered shopping centers? This is a no-brainer. I mean, why stroll safely from store to store in bad weather under one climate-controlled roof, able to periodically rest on a bench or get a snack, when you can, instead, dodge cars under the hot sun or in the blinding snow while crossing complex, low-visibility parking lots?

Tech Solutions: Gadgets and Gizmos

Most of the advice in this book is decidedly low tech. Still, high-tech solutions for home health get headlines because they're intriguing and because technology has long been sold as the greatest problem-solver ever. Current home-health technologies may have their best application to long-distance caregiving, advanced memory loss, serious physical disability and the isolation of living alone. Given the widespread nature of these problems, new technologies are worth a look. Just remember that technology is not *necessarily* the first, best or only solution to a problem.

So here's a brief overview of some current and emerging options. To learn more, visit the Center for Aging Services Technologies (www.agingtech.org), a program of Leading Age, formerly the American Association of Homes and Services for the Aging. The Clearinghouse section will lead you to currently available products and pilot programs.

Among the more tried-and-true technologies are emergency response systems, which may be a very good idea for older people living alone. Here are some useful guidelines for their use. (Excerpted from *How to Care for Aging Parents*, Copyright ©1996, 2004 by Virginia Morris. Used by permission of Workman Publishing Co., New York. All Rights Reserved.)

— ◆ —

The emergency response system provides your parent with a help button, which can be worn as a pendant or on a wrist band. At the response center your parent is identified by a code. If she falls, has chest pains, or needs help for any reason, she pushes the button which triggers her telephone to automatically dial a response center. The center will then call 911 or will phone your parent. If your parent cannot get to the phone, the responder talks with her through a two-way intercom that is attached to the phone. If she doesn't respond to the call or says that there is, indeed, an emergency, the responder then calls an emergency crew.

Dozens of companies now sell emergency response systems. You can find them in the Yellow Pages or on the Internet under "emergency response system," or check with a medical supply store. Or you can ask your parent's doctor if the hospital he is affiliated with offers such a service.

Prices vary, so call several companies. Some sell the system . . . and then charge a monthly service fee. Others rent systems. . . . Still other companies lease systems for a set time. Renting and leasing are often preferable because you don't have to worry about repairs or a company going defunct or moving. Hospitals and social service organizations sometimes offer the systems for free or at a discount to people living on low incomes.

When comparing systems, [remember to] ask for details about the staff receiving emergency calls. Are they available twenty-four hours a day, seven days a week? How are they trained? Do they speak your parent's native language? Find out the company's average response time (if they are not checking their response time periodically, they should be). How often and how does the center test the system to be sure it's working?

Be sure your parent can operate the buttons. Then test the system to see how well it operates within his house and how far he can venture into the backyard, for example, before the system fails.

Ask if your parent can try the system for a trial period or get a money-back guarantee. Find out about warranty, cancellation, service, and repair policies.

◆

Aging-expert Morris concludes her advice with a reminder to test the system and check its batteries regularly. Additionally, because emergency response systems can't cover all possible scenarios (for example, when a parent is in the shower or sleeping, or suddenly becomes confused), Morris notes that it's important to enlist neighbors and any trustworthy people who regularly see your parent, to keep an eye on things and let you know if anything seems wrong.

Going a step further, passive monitoring systems use motion sensors to track activity and send reports to both caregivers and system providers. For example, sensors in high-traffic spots can collect data about whether people get out of bed, stop by a medicine station and stick to their routines. The use of sensors rather than cameras helps people feel more private. Activity changes are analyzed, often by "intelligent" software that "learns" normal routines in order to detect change. Caregivers can monitor the situation by email, cell phone, text message, pager, or password-protected website.

Home devices can also take blood pressure and send the readings to a monitoring center that tells the doctor of any change. If pressure isn't taken daily, the system will notify the doctor, whose office can call in a reminder. Remote devices can also transmit information about weight and breathing.

Futuristic appliances and home systems may offer such features as adjustable display panels, high-contrast readability, alarm volume controls, touch screens and cooktops that can sense cookware heat or sound an alarm if liquid boils over. Today's electric kettles, slow cookers and rice cookers have automatic shutoff.

Meanwhile, hot on the automated heels of the robotic vacuum Roomba, robots are expected to help with other everyday tasks such as running appliances, right down to opening and closing the refrigerator door (which is more than many teenagers can manage).

Mass production may, in time, make robotic aides cheaper than the cost of care by a living, breathing person, although, of course, the skills and companionship are at completely different levels. Already, prototype "nurse-bots" can remind patients to take meds, retrieve small objects, follow people around, call 911 or check vital signs. Their webcams, microphones, speech recognition software, touch-sensitive screens and Internet connections may one day help doctors conduct virtual house calls or let family members check in from afar.

Inventive minds are also looking at everything from shoe insoles that sense balance and signal when a person falls, to carpets that measure gait changes. Also watch for high-tech enhancements to things we normally wear, such as eyeglasses and watches.

And what of Teresa, whose housework load doubled after her husband died? She was smart about her staying power. She invited her handy relatives and friends to a "Handyman Special" party to help her clean out and organize Anthony's tools. They left her with essentials, showed her how to use them and enjoyed some homemade chili and pasta salad.

During the afternoon, Teresa talked to her closest confidantes about whether they could come over and help with regular chores. She also approached the neighbors to ask how they handled different tasks, learn the costs and reputation of hired help and see if they had teenagers who could mow and shovel for a little pocket money.

LET'S GET STARTED
Top Tips for a Useful Home

____ Clearly label all flammable and toxic items and store away from heat and flame.

____ Use and regularly shake or hose down outdoor rubber mats and runners.

____ Use a boot scraper to remove slippery outdoor debris from footwear.

____ Move the mailbox to a comfortable height.

____ Improve front-door lighting, storage and ease of use (ditto for other frequently used entrance doors, such as the door from the garage to the inside of the house).

____ Light all utility areas correctly (they tend to be dark), and store items off the floor.

____ Replace old or broken appliances with more user-friendly new models.

____ Assess cleaning tools for ease of use.

☑ LET'S GO SHOPPING

Top Tools for a Useful Home

- ☐ Lighted doorbell
- ☐ Peephole
- ☐ Offset door hinges
- ☐ Lever door handles
- ☐ Motion-sensor exterior floodlights
- ☐ Photo-sensitive front-door lamps or timer controls
- ☐ New back-friendly snow shovels
- ☐ Small bags of rock salt or other ice melting compound
- ☐ Small bag of kitty litter (basic will do)
- ☐ Small table/chair to hold packages at front door
- ☐ Pull-on traction cleats or spikes
- ☐ Rubber-backed bathmat for foyer floor
- ☐ Long-handled dusters
- ☐ Lightweight vacuum cleaners
- ☐ Rolling shopping carts

Chapter 8

The Possible Home: Getting the Job Done

From stair rails to smoke alarms and slip-resistant tiles, simple home modifications can transform a home and boost insight into aging. Now you may be saying to yourself, this is all very interesting, and I would like to increase the staying power of my mother/parents/ neighbors/in-laws/customer/friend/self, but how do I move from theory to application? What to do? Where to start? How to pay?

Not to worry. This chapter will guide you through the process and, together with the Appendix, recommend resources you can consult to go deeper into areas of special concern, as well as lead you to the tangible items you may need. If you can make a list, do a little shopping and call a handyman, you can get the job done.

If you're the enterprising type, please note there's a great need for innovative, local nonprofit groups, whether staffed by volunteers or professionals, to help older people repair and maintain their homes at low or no cost. It would be good for them and it would benefit the entire neighborhood in terms of safety, appearance and home values.

Planning Department: First Steps

Approach this as you would any other project. Even if you think you know what you want to do, the process will go smoother if you define the problem first. A careful survey of current needs will lead to the most thoughtful and appropriate solutions.

Effective needs assessments will cover the following areas:

+ *Occupant status:* What can they (we) do? What can't they (we) do? What's getting harder? What are the particular problems? What might change in the next year or two?

+ *Home status:* What works, what doesn't work for these particular people? Is the home owned or rented? How long do they (or we) want to stay in the home?

+ *Project resources:* Is there a budget for home modifications? How much? What are the resources: Who's handy? Who's available? What kinds of outside skills and support might be needed? Who do you have, and who do you need to find? If you don't live in the area, how could you locate expert help?

✦ *Priorities:* Safety first! Tackle fall and fire prevention first without fail. Only then, address individual limitations. Among older people, the biggest needs are typically for modifications that reduce energy demands (cardiovascular conditions), aid mobility and dexterity (arthritis), and increase light levels and quality (vision loss). Still, everybody is different. Let the person be your guide.

Way to Go: Form vs. Function

After you finish the needs assessment, you should have a rough framework for intervention. This will include a general list of needs and sequence for implementation, a list of available and needed resources, and some notes on limiting factors, whether they be cost, time, distance, a multistaircase home or a rental (home changes must be easily reversible).

Organize the project in the way you work best. That's known only to you, whether you like to work with folders, binders, index cards, whiteboards, or on a laptop. The project, which will be ongoing, will take tangible form in one of two ways:

✦ *Function by function:* Focus on fall prevention and fire safety first. Then (for example), for someone in the early stages of macular degeneration who is on a waiting list for knee replacement, tackle vision support (lighting levels, contrast and large print), followed by modified furniture and functional (kitchen/bathroom) equipment to minimize squatting and the need to go up and down.

✦ *Room by room:* kitchen, then washrooms, then bedroom, then leisure space . . .

Although typical decorating projects go room by room, this is no typical decorating project. First, it's being undertaken more for functional and less for aesthetic reasons. Second, the occupants may be more comfortable with change if it's integrated more with home "systems" rather than conducted like a makeover. Third, people live in more than one room; they can fall anywhere (the consequences may be greatest on the stairs or in the bathroom).

In addition, a functional approach can be more efficient and cost-effective. You become an expert by focusing on one topic at a time, which enables you to develop the best possible solution to the problem. You know all the suppliers for that particular project type, allowing you to shop around for cost and quality. By grouping tasks to reduce cost and maximize resources, you need hire only a single contractor or tradesperson one time for modifications or repairs.

For example, an electrician can more easily assess wiring and lighting by working on a comprehensive list of projects than by coming back once every two months to fix a lamp here, a breaker there. And with plumbers, you minimize trip charges.

Inspector Gadget: Making Lists

It's time to make lists, so grab your clipboard or tablet computer. To conduct a basic needs assessment, walk through the home slowly, room by room. With one sheet of paper per room, sorted by topic (for example, vision, mobility, falls, or fires), jot down what must be changed or moved. It will look something like this:

LIVING ROOM

✦ *Falls:* Remove extension cord and scatter rug, replace rocking chair with stable high-back chair.
✦ *Fires:* Remove extension cord.
✦ *Vision:* Add contrasting switch plates, install overhead fixture, add window sheers.

After you're done, you'll have a collection of notes organized first by room and then by function. Now, reorganize the notes and list all the recommendations on new sheets with the opposite organization: topic first, then room. The next step is to star, highlight or otherwise code the recommended actions by their type; for example, buy, do it yourself or hire someone.

Your list will now look something like this:

FALL PREVENTION
Living room:

✦ Remove extension cord *(DIY)*
✦ Remove scatter rug *(DIY)*/sell or toss
✦ Replace rocking chair with stable high-back chair *(sell or move to safer spot/use different chair or buy)*

Foyer:

+ Obtain boot tray *(buy)*
+ Make sign for shoes *(DIY)*
+ Add umbrella stand *(make)*
+ Sturdy chair for packages *(buy)*
+ Wall hooks *(buy/install)*

Kitchen:

+ Post sign about wiping spills *(make and hang)*

Stairs:

+ Remove carpet and refinish *(call Joe, the handyman, or handy relative or friend)*
+ Add traction tape *(DIY)*
+ Install second handrail *(Joe again)*

The next step is to make yet another list, this time sorting everything that needs to happen for fall prevention by action type: DIY, buy, call and so on. For example:

+ *DIY:* remove extension cord, remove scatter rug, remove (sell? donate?) rocking chair or glider, make shoe and spill signs, post signs, make umbrella stand, install traction tape
+ *BUY:* chairs, boot tray, wall hooks, traction tape, umbrella stand supplies
+ *CALL:* Joe about stair carpet and refinishing, handrail. *Handrail first?*

As you can see, for the first or next priority topic, such as fall prevention or low vision, you now have a to-do list, a shopping list and a call list. Next to each task, jot down resources such as contractor names and numbers, potential sources (local shops, online stores) and estimated costs (if any).

Be sure to include estimated time to completion and the time available to undertake the project. *Transfer project task times to your regular calendar.* Without appointed times, these projects run the risk of being bumped to the bottom below the more pressing business of daily life.

That is, until somebody falls. Then it gets urgent. But thanks to you and how you're acting on your magic lists, that possibility just got a whole lot smaller.

Hired Hands: Working With Contractors

As should be clear by now, many minor adjustments can make a big difference in safety and quality of life. These do-it-yourself projects should be enjoyable, mostly low cost and not very time consuming.

Some projects, however, require skilled help. In that case, a trusted carpenter, handyman, plumber or electrician should be able to make the required modifications. Show them the guidelines for installing grab bars. If you're still in the brainstorming stage, review books and websites about accessible design (see the Appendix for some titles) to get ideas and present what seem to be the most feasible ones to the carpenter or contractor.

To hire a new contractor, regardless of project type or customer age, follow the standard guidelines. The National Consumers League cautions homeowners to get multiple estimates on home repair projects before signing contracts, check references and, if possible, visit other job sites to check work quality. Make sure the contractor is bonded and insured. Check for complaints with the Better Business Bureau and also whether the contractor is licensed and registered with the local board of contractors and building inspection office.

The League also counsels consumers never to pay in full up front, especially for cash-only deals. And, of course, it reminds people to document in writing the scope of the work to be done and the entire cost and time necessary to complete the job and how payment will be handled.

Homeowners are rightly cautioned to beware of contractors who sell door to door, saying they're "working in the neighborhood." Isn't it funny how many "roofers" appear in the wake of a tornado or hurricane?

Reject anyone who talks too fast, presents slick and scary marketing materials (*"your house will cave in if you don't line your crawl space with NASA-approved titanium sheathing"*), or pressures you into signing on the spot. Some of these scammers tell customers to pay for everything up front, and some of these guys take only cash. One was known to drive an overly trusting older woman to her bank so she could take out the cash on the spot!

Because fraudsters go after old people (see Chapter 6 for more about elder fraud), AARP offers additional recommendations (adapted from *Home Modification: Your Key to Comfort, Safety, and Independent Living*):

1. *List what you want to have done in exact detail.* For example, I keep a running list for our contractor on the computer and give him a hard copy so he can check things off as he goes. It gives us a shared list for preparing and reviewing itemized bills.

2. *Get recommendations from family, friends and neighbors.* Ask about the price, time and quality of workmanship. Local hardware and home improvement stores may have recommendations as well; the large chains send their own contract installers.

3. *Check references.* Ask for names and contact information for previous customers. See if there are complaints on file with the local Better Business Bureau and state Consumer Protection Office (see the Appendix for links). Check licensing, the minimum qualification for a contractor.

4. *Compare contractors.* Find out how long they've been in business and ask for proof that they're licensed, bonded and covered by workers' compensation and liability insurance.

5. *Get estimates.* Meet with at least three contenders to discuss the job and get written estimates, which should include the materials they'll use, labor charges, start and end dates, and total cost.

6. *Get a clear and detailed written contract.* Don't approve any plans unless you understand them. Before you sign, take your time and get a second

opinion. Never sign a contract with blank spaces, and get a copy of everything you sign.

7. *Don't pay the final bill until all the work is done and you are satisfied, the site is clean, and local building authorities inspect the work (if required).* Get written warranties for materials and workmanship, as well as a statement that the contractor has paid all subcontractors and suppliers.

Pay Pals: Cost Containment

Rearranging the furniture costs nothing. Taking off bifocals for going down the stairs is free. Light bulbs, boot trays, traction tape and a new can opener are not major expenses. Slipcovers and stair rails are still in the moderate range. Larger projects and renovations, however, may be more difficult for people living on fixed incomes.

The first rule of bargain shopping is to get only what you need. The second rule of bargain shopping is to get the best quality possible on your budget. To satisfy those rules, answer some questions before you buy:

+ What do the residents' doctors and other health-care providers think is needed?
+ Which health- and safety-related items are really necessary? Which ones will quickly become obsolete? What are the priorities?
+ How do prices compare between vendors? If one vendor's price is a lot cheaper, is it due to lower quality? Is the bargain really a bargain?

◆ What about warranties and guarantees? Will the vendor replace defective items, or do they have to be sent back to the manufacturer? Is that possible in this situation?

The AARP *Home Modifications* booklet and website offers additional advice on financing and paying for home modifications. To summarize its cautions, avoid pressure to finance through a particular company, especially one linked to the contractor. Get several independent estimates for financing and ask a lawyer or housing counselor to explain what it means. Many states allow homeowners to cancel a repair contract by sending a letter within three business days if the contract was signed somewhere other than the contractor's permanent place of business.

Any suspicion of fraud should be called to the attention of the police, the local consumer protection agency, the state attorney general or provincial ministry of consumer services or consumer protection, and the local office of banking. A lawyer can advise you if it's possible to sue the contractor or lender in this circumstance.

Local housing agencies may provide resources. Federal programs, such as the HOME program or Community Development Block Grants, may be available for local housing needs, including home modifications and repair.

In Canada, the Home Adaptations for Seniors' Independence (HASI) Program may be able to help lower-income seniors. More extensive projects, such as widening halls and doorways, might be eligible under the Residential Rehabilitation Assistance Program for Persons With Disabilities. Details for both programs are available on the Canada Mortgage and Housing Corporation's website (www.cmhc-schl.gc.ca).

Here's another idea: To help defray costs, ask whether a local service organization, school carpentry class or carpenters union would like to build a ramp or install pocket doors (for example) as a public-service project. The Village to Village Network (see the Appendix) enlarges upon this idea by providing support for locally driven volunteer services for aging in place.

Regulations and Taxes

Most projects in this book don't require consulting the local authorities about the building code. However, major projects undertaken for whatever reason are expected to conform to code. Before making major structural changes or external alterations (such as a ramp), check with the local municipality. Codes can vary from city to city or province to province, so it's important to start at the local level. The department in question might be called the building or housing department. Most building codes are now posted on the Internet. Local authorities can also inform you about zoning regulations that could affect larger projects.

Licensed contractors, such as builders, electricians and plumbers, are expected to conform to code. Home inspectors are expected to know current codes as well. Still, it doesn't hurt to double-check with the relevant authority. It's costly and painful to make a change, only to have an inspector drop by and tell you to try again.

Home Game: Age-Proof Staying Power

Are you ready to age-proof? The tips and tricks in this book will get you started, whether you plan to spend a couple of weekends helping out your parents or want to undertake some long-term planning for yourself. The Appendix contains additional resources to help you learn about aging and support a safe and satisfying passage through the years.

As a final measure, give some thought to your people resources. Who is going to check in on your parents when you can't? People in this situation can arrange with grown children, other family members, friends or neighbors to check on one another regularly. Adult children can also trade names and numbers of parents' close friends and neighbors. Community support is the ultimate security.

Is age-proofing worth the weekends you might spend making lists and shopping around, as well as the time it takes to organize, supervise or make small modifications?

Definitely!

First, as this book has demonstrated, it's relatively easy to help yourself and other people to master domestic life as the years go on. Second, although we may never know the accidents that might have happened if we did not intervene, every day without a fall or fire is a good day—free for something better. Third, it can be deeply gratifying to help folks of any age stay healthy and use their time and talents to the fullest.

So what are you waiting for? Age-proof that home . . . pump up your Staying Power!

Appendix

Resources and Recommended Reading

AGING AND CAREGIVING

A Long Bright Future: Happiness, Health and Financial Security in an Age of Increased Longevity
Laura L. Carstensen, Ph.D.
Broadway Books

Administration on Aging (AoA)
www.aoa.gov
(202) 619-0724 (public inquiries)
Federal agency offering support through information, referral and outreach on the local level

Area Agencies on Aging
www.n4a.org
(202) 872-0888
Website includes directory of state resources for staying at home as long as possible. Click "Consumer" link on top of screen.

Coping With Your Difficult Older Parent: A Guide for Stressed-Out Children
Grace Lebow and Barbara Kane, with Irwin Lebow
Avon Books

Doing the Right Thing: Taking Care of Your Elderly Parents, Even If They Didn't Take Care of You
Roberta Satow
Jeremy P. Tarcher/Penguin

Eldercare 911: The Caregiver's Complete Handbook for Making Decisions
Susan Beerman and Judith Rappaport-Musson
Prometheus Books

Eldercare Locator
www.eldercare.gov
(800) 677-1116
A service of the AoA that connects people to services for older adults and their families

Happiness is Growing Old at Home: Discover New Ways to Help Your Aging Parent Remain Independent
Maria Tadd
Terrapin Press

How to Care for Aging Parents
Virginia Morris
Workman Publishing

National Association of Professional Geriatric Care Managers
www.caremanager.org
Private health and human service specialists who help families care for older relatives; includes a database searchable by location

National Institute on Aging
www.nia.nih.gov
(301) 496-1752
Includes http://nihseniorhealth.gov, an easy-to-use, accommodating website with health and wellness information for older adults

Seniors Canada Online
www.seniors.gc.ca
(800) 622-6232
Government-provided information and programs for older adults; see also www.seniorsinfo.ca

The Senior Organizer: Personal, Medical, Legal, Financial
Debby S. Bitticks, Lynn Benson and
Dorothy K. Breininger
Health Communications

This Caring Home
http://thiscaringhome.org

Online expert tips and tools to enhance home safety for persons with Alzheimer's and other forms of dementia

Village to Village Network
www.vtvnetwork.org

Grassroots network of local, membership-driven services for aging in place, with interactive map showing member "villages"

ASSISTIVE DEVICES AND HOME MODIFICATION

The AARP Home Fit Guide
http://assets.aarp.org/www.aarp.org_/articles/livable_
communities/aarp_home_fit_guide_042010.pdf

Additional safety and energy-saving tips for older adults

AbleData
www.abledata.com

(800) 227-0216

Federally* funded database of assistive products and manufacturers has information specialists to help callers; detailed descriptions of thousands of products, including price and company information

---

*State assistive technology projects can also be accessed through AbleData

The Accessible Home: Updating Your Home for Changing Physical Needs

Editors of Creative Publishing International
Creative Publishing International

Especially good for the do-it-yourself type

Accessibility Professionals Inc.

www.accessible-kitchens.com/
www.accessible-bathrooms.com/

A network of providers that help people age in place; positive images of disability and home modifications

Accessible Housing by Design—Ramps

Canadian Mortgage and Housing Corporation
www.cmhc-schl.gc.ca/en/co/renoho/refash/refash_025.cfm

Detailed design and construction advice for portable, modular and site-constructed ramps

American Occupational Therapy Association

www.aota.org/Consumers/consumers/Adults/AginginPlace/Home

Fact sheet: "Helping Your Older Parent Remain at Home"

http://www.aota.org/Consumers/consumers/Adults/AginginPlace/Home

General resources on aging: arthritis, low vision, fall prevention and more

Association of Assistive Technology Act Programs
www.ataporg.org

e-pill Medication Reminders
www.epill.com

More than 50 different reminder devices, including tamper-proof and monitored systems

Environmental Geriatrics Program
Cornell University
www.environmentalgeriatrics.com

✦ *Grab bar guidelines:* www.environmentalgeriatrics.com/ pdf/handouts/grab_bars.pdf

✦ *Decluttering guidelines pertinent to hoarding:* www.environmentalgeriatrics.com/home_safety/ decluttering.html

Home Adaptations for Seniors' Independence Program (HASI)
Canadian Mortgage and Housing Corporation
www.cmhc-schl.gc.ca/en/ab/noho/noho_006.cfm

Helps low-income homeowners and landlords pay for minor home adaptations

Home Modification: Your Key to Comfort, Safety, and Independent Living
AARP
www.aarp.org
(888) OUR-AARP (888-687-2277)

The Illustrated Guide to Assistive Technology & Devices: Tools and Gadgets for Living Independently
Suzanne Robitaille
Demos Medical Publishing

National Association of Home Builders
www.nahb.org/
(800) 368-5242
Trains builders as Certified Aging in Place Specialists (CAPS) to remodel homes for aging; website has online directory of CAPS

The National Resource Center on Supportive Housing and Home Modification
www.homemods.org
(213) 740-1364
Database of local programs and contractors who specialize in home modifications and will do other maintenance work for seniors at a discount
www.homemods.org/directory/index.shtml

Preventing Falls on Stairs
Canadian Mortgage and Housing Corp.
www.cmhc-schl.gc.ca/en/co/maho/adse/adse_001.cfm

Public Health Agency of Canada, Division of Aging and Seniors

www.phac-aspc.gc.ca/seniors-aines

(613) 952-7606

With links to download PDF documents, including:

✦ *Go for It! A Guide to Choosing and Using Assistive Devices*

✦ *Help Yourself to Assistive Devices!*

Shared Solutions America: Livable Homes

www.livablehomes.org

Resource Center for education, technology, and funding alternatives for seniors and people of all ages with disabilities; see detailed checklists for home adaptations at www.livablehomes.org/checklist.html

COGNITIVE AGING AND ALZHEIMER'S DISEASE

Alzheimer's Disease Education & Referral Center (ADEAR Center)

www.alzheimers.org

(800) 438-4380

Free information; sign up for email news about important findings and to participate in research studies

The Alzheimer's Action Plan: What You Need to Know—and What You Can Do—About Memory Problems, From Prevention to Early Intervention and Care
P. Murali Doraiswamy, M.D., and Lisa P. Gwyther, M.S.W., with Tina Adler
St. Martin's Press

The Complete Guide to Alzheimer's Proofing Your Home (Revised Edition)
Mark Warner and Ellen Warner
Purdue University Press

The 36-Hour Day: A Family Guide to Caring for Persons With Alzheimer Disease, Related Dementing Illnesses, and Memory Loss In Later Life
Nancy L. Mace, M.A., and Peter V. Rabins, M.D., M.P.H.
Warner Books

DESIGN FOR AGING

AARP
www.aarp.org
(888) 687-2277
How to make homes user-friendly for people with disabilities at www.aarp.org/families/home_design

AARP Guide to Revitalizing Your Home: Beautiful Living for the Second Half of Life
Rosemary Bakker
Lark Books

Access by Design
George A. Covington and Bruce Hannah
Van Nostrand Reinhold

Elder Design: Designing and Furnishing a Home for Your Later Years
Rosemary Bakker
Penguin Books

Residential Design for Aging in Place
Drue Lawlor and Michael Thomas
Wiley

The Senior Cohousing Handbook, 2nd Edition: A Community Approach to Independent Living
Charles Durrett
New Society Publishers

Unassisted Living: Ageless Homes for Later Life
Jeffrey P. Rosenfeld and Wid Chapman
The Monacelli Press

Universal Design for the Home: Great-Looking, Great-Living Design for All Ages, Abilities and Circumstances
Wendy A. Jordan
Quarry Books

FITNESS OVER 50

American College of Sports Medicine
www.acsm.org
(317) 637-9200

American Council on Exercise
www.acefitness.org
(888) 825-3636

Arthritis Foundation
www.arthritis.org
(800) 283-7800

American Heart Association
www.americanheart.org
(800) AHA-USA-1
Go to "Getting Healthy" tab for resources on physical activity

Canadian Centre for Activity and Aging
www.uwo.ca/actage
(519) 661-2111

Centers for Disease Control and Prevention

Physical Activity for Everyone

Web-based guidelines and videos

www.cdc.gov/physicalactivity/everyone/guidelines/
olderadults.html

Exercise: A Guide From the National Institute on Aging

Publication No. NIH 99-4258

www.nih.gov/nia

(800) 222-2225

Go4Life Exercise Campaign: National Institute on Aging

http://go4life.niapublications.org/

Exercise & Activity: Your Everyday Guide and exercise DVD are available free to U.S. residents

Health Canada's Physical Activity Guide for Healthy Living

www.phac-aspc.gc.ca/hp-ps/hl-mvs/pa-ap/08paap-eng.php

Heart and Stroke Foundation of Canada

Use "Health Information" tab, go to "Healthy Living," then "Physical Activity"

www.heartandstroke.ca

(613) 569-4361

Mayo Clinic Fitness for Everybody
Diane Dahm, M.D., and Jay Smith, M.D.
Mayo Clinic Health Information

Spark: The Revolutionary New Science of Exercise and the Brain
John J. Ratey, M.D., with Eric Hagerman
Little, Brown and Co.

Strength Training Over 50
D. Cristine Caivano
Barron's

HOME HEALTH EQUIPMENT
(This list is for information only and does not imply endorsement.)

Agecomfort.com
www.agecomfort.com
Canadian online store for healthcare products

The Alzheimer's Store
www.alzstore.com
(800) 752-3238

CVS Pharmacy Home Health
www.cvs.com/homehealth

Drive Medical
www.drivemedical.com
(877) 224-0946

Elderluxe
www.elderluxe.com
(888) 537-LUXE
Mobility products, fitness equipment, elder tools

Functional Solutions
www.beabletodo.com
(800) 235-7054

Gold Violin
www.goldviolin.com
(877) 648-8400

Independent Living Aids
www.independentliving.com
(800) 537-2118

Maddak
www.maddak.com
(973) 628-7600

North Coast Medical
www.ncmedical.com
(800) 821-9319

Patterson Medical
www.pattersonmedical.com or www.pattersonmedical.ca

(800) 323-5547 (U.S.) or (800) 665-9200 (Canada)

Rexall
www.rexall.ca

ShoppersHomeHealthCare
www.shoppersdrugmart.ca/english/home_health_care/

Walgreens
www.walgreens.com

Home Health Care Solutions tab

The Wright Stuff
www.thewright-stuff.com

(877) 750-0376

"Health Care Products That Make Life Easier"

HOME SAFETY AND FRAUD

AARP
www.aarp.org/money/scams-fraud/

Better Business Bureau
http://lookup.bbb.org

Canadian Anti-Fraud Centre
www.antifraudcentre-centreantifraude.ca/

Canadian Bankers Association "Financial Abuse: What Seniors Need to Know"

www.cba.ca/en/consumer-information/42-safeguarding-your-money/483-financial-abuse-what-seniors-need-to-know

Consumer Protection Office (by state)

http://consumeraction.gov/state.shtm

Fall Prevention Center of Excellence

www.stopfalls.org

National Consumers League: National Fraud Information Center

✦ "They Can't Hang Up: Five Steps to Help Seniors Targeted by Telemarketing Fraud"
www.fraud.org/elderfraud/hangup.htm

✦ "My Do Not Call Registration Information: A Guide to Track Telemarketing Calls"
www.fraud.org/elderfraud/

✦ "Top 10 Red Flags of Home Repair Scams"
www.nclnet.org

Search on "home repair scams"

National Crime Prevention Council: Senior Fraud

www.ncpc.org/newsroom/current-campaigns/senior-fraud

"Seniors and Telemarketing Fraud 101" booklet
www.ncpc.org/resources/files/pdf/fraud/senfraud_rev4.pdf

Net Literacy Senior Connects
www.netliteracy.org

Student volunteers offer free Internet training at senior centers, retirement apartments and independent-living facilities

Public Health Agency of Canada, Division of Aging and Seniors
www.phac-aspc.gc./ca/seniors-aines OR
http://www.publichealth.gc.ca/seniors

(613) 952-7606

Noteworthy publications:
+ *The Safe Living Guide: A Guide to Home Safety for Seniors*
+ *You CAN Prevent Falls!*
+ *12 Steps to Stair Safety*

SeniorNet
www.seniornet.org

Nonprofit organization specializing in computer and Internet education for older adults

LOW VISION AND HEARING

American Foundation for the Blind
www.afb.org

(800) AFB-LINE

American Printing House for the Blind
www.aph.org

(800) 223-1839 (U.S. and Canada)

Source of the MotionPAD motion-activated voice reminder system and other products

Canadian Federation of the Blind
www.cfb.ca

(800) 619-8789

Canadian National Institute for the Blind
www.cnib.ca

(800) 563-2642

Harris Communications
www.harriscomm.com

Voice: (800) 825-6758; TTY: (800) 825-9187

Video Phone: (866) 789-3468 (M–F 9–4 CST)

Fax: (952) 906-1099

Products for deaf and hard-of-hearing people

Hearmore
www.hearmore.com

(800) 881-4327

TTY: (800) 281-3555

Video Phone: (631) 752-1145

Fax: (631) 752-0689

Lighthouse International (including the National Association for Visually Handicapped)

www.lighthouse.org

(800) 829-0500

LS&S

www.lssproducts.com

(800) 468-4789

"Learning, sight & sound made easier"

National Federation of the Blind

www.nfb.org

(410) 659-9314

U.S. Fire Safety Administration/FEMA

Fire safety for the deaf or hard of hearing; includes downloadable information sheet

www.usfa.fema.gov/citizens/disability/fswy19.shtm

Index

Acknowledgments

Folks, you can't make this stuff up. For sharing their knowledge and wisdom, I thank above all the faculty of the University of North Carolina (UNC) Institute on Aging.

And thank you as well to the many experts who reviewed portions of the manuscript with care:

+ Shelly Agarwal, Lighthouse International
+ Janis Blenden, geriatric care manager, Broward County, Florida
+ John Breyault, National Consumers League
+ Jena Ivey Burkhart, UNC Eshelman School of Pharmacy, UNC Hospitals and Clinics
+ Debra Drelich, New York Elder Care Consultants LLC
+ Beth Gould, registered dietitian, Richmond Hill, Ontario
+ David Hart, M.D., scientific director, The Arthritis Society of Canada
+ Sydelle Rose Hoffman, EatPlayHug.com
+ Janice Johnstone, Office of the Fire Marshal, Ontario, Canada

+ Julian Keith, University of North Carolina, Wilmington
+ Ona McDonald, CanFitPro Pro Trainer, Markham, Ontario
+ Christine Mazzola Khandelwal, UNC Health Care Center for Aging and Health
+ Ron Moldenhauer, Barrier Free Homes (www. barrierfreehomeplans.com)
+ Larry Parker, D.D.S., Hillcrest Orthodontics, Richmond Hill, Ontario
+ Jackson Roush, Division of Speech and Hearing Sciences, UNC School of Medicine
+ Victor Schoenbach, Department of Epidemiology, UNC Gillings School of Global Public Health
+ Karen Smith, American Occupational Therapy Association
+ Martha Wolf, Alzheimer Center, Parker Jewish Institute for Health Care & Rehabilitation

Gifted people taught me how we relate to our physical world. They include Bill Korbus, professor emeritus of the School of Journalism, University of Texas at Austin; Ben Shneiderman, founding director of the Human-Computer Interaction Laboratory at the University of Maryland, College Park; Darren Tenn of Tenn Renovations in Markham, Ontario; and Chuck Hollander of CDH Renovations in Raleigh, North Carolina.

My editor, Marla Markman of Markman Editorial Services, was immeasurably helpful. Her high level of competence and knowledge helped make the process of writing this book strangely relaxing.

Thanks to Valerie Holt of Accessibility Professionals, Errol Seef and Sunanda Mongia of Cardinal Health Canada and Courtney Carrasco of ShelfGenie for help with photographs.

Friends, family members and associates in the United States and Canada have been wonderful supporters and sounding boards. Here's to you who lent your insights, whether you knew it or not.

From A to Zed: Nenette Adelson-Rodriguez, Katharine Andriotis and Laura Hays, Karen Beimdiek Baratz, Chuck Boyer, Juanita Carmi, Cheryl Crosby, Belinda Dowdy, Sally Fessler, Gerry and Sheila Gafka, Marie Lehman (who shared her illustrator talents as well), Kaestner and Jackie McDonnough, Tia Marsh, Barbara Meyers, Sharon Mills, Barbara Morris, Jennifer and Roger Pyke, Cyndy Ratcliffe, Susan and Scott Orshan, Karen Priesman, Sheldon and Beth Rose, Stephanie Scotti and Gay Slesinger.

Alan Breznick, my husband, read everything at least three times, offered indispensable advice and fixed the commas. Pamela Breznick, our daughter, helped me with my studies and never begrudged the time it took to get this done.

Our elders, Hazel Adelson, Saul Breznick and Edith Breznick, have taught us about aging at home with grace, stoicism and economy.

Humble thanks to anyone I overlooked. It must have been a senior moment.

About the Author

Pamela Breznick

Rachel Adelson, M.A., is a science writer specializing in health and aging.

After a successful career as an editor, speechwriter and program manager with IBM, she founded Live Wire Communications to help clients in the health, science and technology sectors. Notable clients have included IBM, AT&T, American Psychological Association, National Multiple Sclerosis Society, Discovery Communications, Baycrest Centre for Geriatric Care, and Ontario's Central Community Care Access Centre (CCAC). Her writing has merited two National Health Information Awards and a Women in Communications Clarion Award.

Rachel has covered everything from brain health and neurological disorders to behavioral economics and human-computer interaction. Her curiosity has led her to projects as diverse as writing a column on computer confidence, researching how people communicate about Alzheimer's disease, and certifying to teach fitness to older adults—a task that put both her knees and her knowledge to the test.

She has a master's degree in journalism, a bachelor's degree in psychology and graduate certificates in aging and public health.

A native of New York City, Rachel has called Texas, Maryland and North Carolina home. She lives with her family outside Toronto and does indeed put friction tape on the stairs.

Learn more about Rachel Adelson at
www.racheladelson.com.

57995053R00149

Made in the USA
San Bernardino, CA
25 November 2017